# Language Experience Approach to Reading (and Writing)

# LANGUAGE EXPERIENCE APPROACH to READING (and WRITING)

## Language-Experience Reading for Second Language Learners

Carol N. Dixon • Denise Nessel

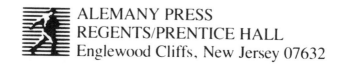

ALEMANY PRESS
REGENTS/PRENTICE HALL
Englewood Cliffs, New Jersey 07632

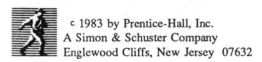
Printed in the United States of America
10 9 8 7 6 5 4 3 2

ISBN   0-13-521352-5

Prentice-Hall International (UK) Limited, *London*
Prentice-Hall of Australia Pty. Limited, *Sydney*
Prentice-Hall Canada Inc., *Toronto*
Prentice-Hall Hispanoamericana, S. A., *Mexico*
Prentice-Hall of India Private Limited, *New Delhi*
Prentice-Hall of Japan, Inc., *Tokyo*
Simon & Schuster Asia Pte. Ltd., *Singapore*
Editora Prentice-Hall do Brasil, Ltda., *Rio de Janeiro*

# Acknowledgements

We thank the following ESL teachers, who generously shared ideas with us and gave us copies of their students' work to include in this book.

Barbara Clark
Sandra Coopersmith-Beezy
Millie Farnum
Elida Flores
Joan Hahn
Linda La Puma
Cheryl Morgan
Doug Parham
Sara Sanchez
Matilda Sanchez-Villalpando
Nancy Shibata
Katherine Shoenrock
Lydia Swanson
Simon Unzuerta

We also thank Roger Olsen for his valuable suggestions and encouragement, and Russell Stauffer who taught us to honor our students' language and experiences.

# *Table of Contents*

*To*
*Jim and Ed*

# Introduction

The Language Experience Approach (LEA) to reading instruction is not a new idea. It has been documented and discussed since early this century (Huey, 1908; Smith, 1967). Adaptations and variations have been explored and described by many. Sylvia Ashton-Warner's key word concept (Ashton-Warner, 1963) and Doris Lee's chart stories (Lamoreaux and Lee, 1943) are only two examples of educators using basic LEA principles to help students learn to read. Reading experts have generally considered some form of LEA to be basic methodology for teaching reading, and teacher education textbooks have recommended its use (Wilson and Hall, 1972; Spache and Spache, 1977; Stauffer, 1980).

In all its forms the central LEA concept remains the same — use the student's own vocabulary, language patterns, and background of experiences to create the reading text and make reading a meaningful process. The usual LEA techniques (Stauffer, 1980; Nessel and Jones, 1981) involve these steps:

Step 1    Teacher and students discuss the stimulus, or topic for dictation. Observations and opinions are exchanged. Oral language skills are developed and reinforced.

Step 2    The student dictates an account (the story)* to the teacher, who records the statements to construct the basic reading material.

Step 3    The student reads the story several times, with teacher help as needed, until the story has become quite familiar. Comprehension is assured because the student is reading material that is self-generated.

---

*We use the term *story* to mean any dictated account, whether a fanciful narrative or a factual account of something the learner has experienced.

Step 4   Individual story words are learned, and other reading skills are reinforced through teacher-designed activities related to the story.

Step 5   Students move from reading their own dictation to reading other-author materials as they develop confidence and skill with the reading process.

In all LEA programs, whatever variations might occur at each step, students talk about personal and familiar experiences, and their statements are used to help them acquire the ability to understand written language — to read. Discussion prior to dictation develops and encourages oral skills. Students learn to read using material uniquely suited to their needs and interests, material they have composed orally. Motivation for reading their own stories is high. Recognizing their own words in print is easier than dealing with the unfamiliar language of many readers and textbooks. Eventual transfer to other-author materials can be made comfortably, given the strong base of reading-for-meaning established with the use of dictated stories. The individualized nature of LEA programs allows each teacher to suit instruction to the specific needs and interests of the students.

Rather than using the Language Experience Approach, however, schools have usually chosen basal reader approaches to reading. Basal packages have been presented as safe, well-controlled systems for teaching reading. The materials are backed by experts who serve as program consultants, and detailed scope and sequence charts appear to provide systematic instruction. Most important, the teachers' guides and program components make for an organized approach to planning and conducting lessons. For busy teachers with large classes, the basal approach has seemed preferable to designing an individualized program such as LEA.

While basal readers remain popular, recent theoretical and practical considerations have generated new interest in LEA. Linguists have argued for meaningful input as a prerequisite for language acquisition (Krashen, 1981; Krashen and Terrell, 1983). Psycholinguists have focused attention on the relationship between language acquisition and reading (Goodman and Fleming, 1968; Shuy, 1977). Researchers and theoreticians began suggesting that reading would be easier when the reading text closely matched the learner's own experiences and oral language patterns (Tierney, Readence, and Dishner, 1980). These works provide theoretical justification for choosing LEA as a reading method. At the same time, in the practical world of schools, teachers have been faced with wave after wave of new students from other cultures whose language and experiences have little, if anything, in common with the characters in basal readers. Published American texts and readers have had little relevance to those recently arrived from Asia, Latin America, or other non-English-speaking areas. For these practical reasons many teachers are turning to LEA to help learners with these special problems. Recently, teacher education materials have also specifically recommended using some form of LEA with these students (Ching, 1976; Ransom, 1978).

This text will introduce, or re-acquaint, teachers with the Language Experience Approach, a natural way of helping learners acquire oral, aural, reading, and writing skills, one particularly suited to the needs of the student for whom English is a second language.

*Carol N. Dixon and Denise Nessel*

# REFERENCES

Ashton-Warner, S. *Teacher.* New York: Simon and Schuster, 1963.

Ching, D. C. *Reading and the Bilingual Child.* Newark, DE: International Reading Association, 1976.

Goodman, K., and Fleming, J., (Eds.). *Psycholinguistics and the Teaching of Reading.* Newark, DE: International Reading Association, 1968.

Huey, E. B. *The Psychology and Pedagogy of Reading.* New York: Macmillian, 1908.

Krashen, S. D. *Second Language Acquisition.* Oxford: The Pergamon Press, 1981.

Krashen, S. D., and Terrell, T. D. *The Natural Approach.* San Francisco: The Alemany Press, 1983.

Lamoreaux, L., and Lee, D. M. *Learning to Read Through Experiences.* New York: Appleton-Century-Crofts, 1943.

Nessel, D. D., and Jones, M. B. *The Language-Experience Approach to Reading: A Handbook for Teachers.* New York: Teachers College Press, 1981.

Ransom, G. *Preparing to Teach Reading.* Boston: Little, Brown, 1978.

Shuy, R., (Ed.). *Linguistic Theory: What Can It Say About Reading?* Newark, DE: International Reading Association, 1967.

Smith, N. B. *American Reading Instruction.* Newark, DE: International Reading Association, 1967.

Spache, G. E. and Spache, E. B. *Reading in the Elementary School.* Boston: Allyn and Bacon, 1977.

Stauffer, R. G. *The Language Experience Approach to the Teaching of Reading.* New York: Harper and Row, 1980.

Tierney, R. J., Readence, J. E., and Dishner, E. K. *Reading Strategies and Practices: A Guide for Improving Instruction.* Boston: Allyn and Bacon, 1980.

Wilson, R. M. and Hall, M. *Reading and the Elementary School Child.* New York: D. Van Nostrand, 1972.

# Chapter 1

# The Value of LEA for ESL Learners

We use LEA with ESL (English as a Second Language) students because it makes sense as a method and because it works. It makes sense because it is based on what is known about acquiring language and learning to read. It works because, as a flexible, individualized approach, it meets the unique needs of the ESL learner.

## LANGUAGE ACQUISITION AND READING

Recent studies suggest that the process of language acquisition has several characteristics which cut across all language and cultural barriers (Brown, R., 1973; Asher, 1977; Brown, H.D., 1979; Krashen, 1981; Krashen and Terrell, 1983). First (native) languages are acquired in informal, non-academic settings through real life, non-threatening interactions with others, such as family and friends. In fact, acquisition actually slows or even stops altogether in settings where the learner is constantly corrected or reprimanded for incorrect speech. Language is best acquired in settings where there is a need to know, the chance to try, and the freedom to fail without penalty. Once oral language is acquired, the basis for learning to read has been established. Learning to read is an extension of the language learning process.

Second language acquisition may seem a very different matter, yet research has shown that several principles are just as true for acquiring a second language as they are for acquiring a first (Nelson, 1973; Asher, 1977; La Puma, 1980; Krashen, 1981; Krashen and Terrell, 1983). Second language acquisition also takes place most effectively in informal, real life settings where the learner is freely interacting with fluent speakers of the target language. The learner must also have many opportunities to listen to the language without being forced to respond. And, when learners must use the new language, they need to do so naturally, in a supportive, non-threatening environment with the freedom to make mistakes, just as the infant can say "me bottle" without fear of reproach.

These principles of second language acquisition are applicable to second language reading. Learning to read a second language is best accomplished when the reading materials are based on real life experiences that are meaningful to the learner. The student needs many opportunities to practice reading in settings which are both comfortable and designed to promote success, and where errors are regarded as an acceptable part of the process.

## THE LEARNER'S NEEDS

ESL learners share some common characteristics despite the diversity of their cultural and language backgrounds. Most, if not all, are in confusing and often frightening situations. Their native language, on which they have learned to depend, is no longer adequate. They must learn a new system of sounds and symbols which may be radically different from those they have previously known.* In fact, they may lack the ability even to discriminate some American sounds from others. Using English can be an ego-shattering task for the learner who has trouble hearing the sounds of language. When physical existence and that of loved ones depends on accurate speech, life can become terrifying. Not only is the ESL student faced with the disconcerting task of learning another sound/symbol system in order to communicate basic needs, but that same student is also stressed by attempting to understand and acquire a new culture. The fact that the move to the new culture may be accompanied by high hopes for a better life makes it no less difficult. The older the student, the more threatening these changes may be. As a result, the more unwilling such students may become to interact with native speakers, the very behavior which is crucial to learning the new language.

Classrooms for second language students need to approximate natural, real world settings, filled with language. Learners need numerous opportunities to hear fluent English and to interact with fluent English speakers in meaningful situations. Ideally, ESL students at all grade levels will have many opportunities to converse with English-speaking peers. If students are placed in regular classrooms, they will have chances for conversation. If they are placed in special ESL classrooms, every effort must be made to plan times when they can work with and talk with English-speaking peers. When students are encouraged to talk with

*Table 5-1 (page 71) lists several English sounds that are difficult for certain ESL learners.

English-speaking classmates, they will hear many words and phrases over and over. This repetition, which is necessary for language learning, is effective and pleasant because it occurs naturally, in contrast to textbook drills of often meaningless (to the student) phrases and sentences.

ESL learners also need individual practice to refine new language skills. Because they are just learning English, they will make many errors in vocabulary and usage, but these will not be as frustrating if the students are not always expected to perform for the teacher or the whole class. Ideally, these students should have access to practice stations or activity centers to use alone or with a partner. These centers should contain an abundance of films, records, and tapes as additional models of English usage, as well as a wide variety of books, pictures, and objects to stimulate talking, browsing, and reading. Besides many opportunities to practice English, these learners need instruction. The instructional approach needs to increase their total communication skills so that they can use the new language in all communication settings.

## TEACHING FOR COMMUNICATION

The Language Experience Approach has many advantages for the ESL learner because it involves all the communication skills. Dictation is preceded by discussion of the subject or stimulus for the story. The learner has the opportunity both to listen to what others in the group are saying and to participate verbally in the discussion, thereby practicing oral language in a natural communication setting. The dictation itself serves as the basic material for developing reading ability. Once students have begun mastering the reading process through their dictation, writing their own stories is a natural extension.

The reading material—the dictated story—has immediate relevance since it makes use of the learners' own experiences, vocabulary, and language patterns. Attention and motivation remain high, and the learners' self worth is constantly reinforced by the very fact of seeing their own language turned into print. LEA provides ESL students with a meaningful, personally rewarding experience in learning to read English.

The learner's task is made easier and less frustrating because the reading materials match oral language patterns and draw on personal experiences. Learners are not asked to confront unfamiliar or confusing language of texts or readers which are not yet meaningful.

Above all, the Language Experience Approach is one in which the teacher is a facilitator, choosing tasks that will help, not frustrate, the learner. The student is not expected to conform to the demands of a pre-designed program, with unfamiliar characters and language. The teacher plans experiences and activities to meet special learning needs. Language acquisition is promoted when the teacher selects meaningful topics for dictation, thoughtfully guides the discussion before dictation, and encourages the student to use English while dictating the story. Expectations are determined by what the student can do at each stage, not by external standards of performance.

Finally, LEA is an extremely flexible method; there are many variations of the Language Experience Approach. Only one rule remains inviolate—the student's own language is written down to produce the text material for reading instruction. The exact procedures to be followed may be modified in numerous ways to meet individual needs. LEA is well-suited to language learners, allowing, as it does, maximum adjustment to learning needs and minimum threat to self confidence and self worth.

## CHOOSING THE RIGHT APPROACH

ESL learners vary as much in their needs and abilities as any group of students. It is as much a mistake to give all ESL students the same reading program as it is to give any heterogeneous group of learners exactly the same tasks to do and requirements to meet. Of course, a most significant variable among ESL students is English language competence. Assessing that competence is necessary for planning appropriate instruction. Many language assessment tests have been developed, but they do not always provide an accurate picture of the student's total language. Such assessment procedures should be supplemented with observation of the student in natural language settings in order to plan instruction.

The Levels of Use (LoU) model (Hall, Loucks, Rutherford, and Newlove, 1975; Hall and Loucks, 1977) is useful for evaluating acquisition. The LoU was developed to evaluate teachers' abilities to use innovative instructional procedures. The model is based on the recognition that teachers must learn to use an innovative technique, that the learning process takes time, and that teachers will go through predictable stages as they acquire the ability to use the new technique smoothly and efficiently. Although LoU is not intended for evaluating students, we have found the framework useful for looking at language learners, who are, in fact, using an innovative technique — the new language. We have modified the LoU approach to provide a guide for observation and assessment of oral second language acquisition. Our experience suggests (confirmed by Krashen and Terrell, 1983) that there are at least three stages of language acquisition. Table 1-1 summarizes these stages and their respective levels of oral second language use.

*Table 1-1*

**Adapted Levels of Use for Assessing Use of English**

*Stage 1 Student*

| | Level 0: Non-use | Level I: Orientation (Awareness) |
|---|---|---|
| Quantity of oral English | Student has little or no knowledge of English | Student has recently learned a few words of English through incidental daily experiences |
| Ability to use oral English | Student is not using English at all to communicate | Student occasionally understands a single word or phrase of English used by others to communicate |
| Interest in learning additional English | Student is not trying to learn English | Student occasionally attempts to learn the meaning of a new English word used by someone else |

*Stage 2 Student*

| | Level II: Preparation (Investigation) | Level III: Mechanical Use |
|---|---|---|
| Quantity of oral English | Student can understand several English words and phrases | Student can understand and use a vocabulary of stock words and phrases covering many daily situations |
| Ability to use English orally | Student attempts to use a limited number of English words and phrases to communicate basic needs | Student attempts to communicate in English in familiar, non-threatening situations |
| Interest in learning additional English | Student shows interest in understanding new words and phrases related to particular interests or needs | Student is actively seeking to understand new words and phrases through a variety of daily experiences |

*Stage 3 Student*

| | Level IV-A: Routine Use | Level IV-B: Refinement |
|---|---|---|
| Quantity of oral English | Student's language skills are adequate for most day-to-day communication needs in concrete situations | Student understands and uses English correctly except for some idioms, figures of speech, or words with multiple meanings |
| Ability to use English orally | Student is willing to attempt to communicate in English in new or unfamiliar settings if the occasion arises | Student is able to use English successfully in new learning situations |

*Table 1-1 cont.*

|  | *Level IV-A: Routine Use* | *Level IV-B: Refinement* |
|---|---|---|
| Interest in learning additional English | Student shows regular, stable interest in all language improvement activities and lessons | Student actively seeks opportunities to use English in new or unfamiliar settings |

*Students Beyond Stage 3*

Levels V and VI: Integration and Renewal

| | |
|---|---|
| Quantity of oral English | Student understands multiple meanings of words, English idioms and figures of speech |
| Ability to use English orally | Student uses English fluently in all communication settings (listening, speaking, reading, writing) to acquire and manipulate both concrete and abstract ideas |
| Interest in learning additional English | Student actively searches for new English words and meanings, reads a variety of prose forms and attempts a variety of forms in own writing |

Classification into stages depends on students' *ability to use English*, not age or grade in school. LEA can be modified to provide for the needs of students at each stage. The LoU assessment plus knowledge of the students' abilities to read in their native language should be used to choose the most effective language experience variation. Table 1-2 summarizes the major features of each variation for each of the three stages.

*Table 1-2*

**LEA Summary Chart for ESL Students**

|  | Student Characteristics | Instructional Procedures * |
|---|---|---|
| *Stage 1* | almost no oral English and no experience with any written language | key vocabulary; dictated pattern stories |
| *Stage 2* | some oral English and some fluency with written native language | story dictation; structured word lists |
| *Stage 3* | considerable oral English and fluency in oral and written native language | story dictation; story language revision |

* *These procedures may be used for lessons with individual students or for group instruction.*

*Table 1-2 cont.*

|  | Oral language/Dictation Topics | Reading-related Activities |
|---|---|---|
| Stage 1 | student's daily experiences; structured experiences of immediate utility | conversation; role-playing; listening to stories; word discrimination activities |
| Stage 2 | student's daily experiences; American cultural events such as holidays or typical family celebrations; other American customs | read-along books; reader's theater; word recognition activities |
| Stage 3 | student's daily experiences; new areas of learning such as other academic areas; areas of special interest the student is studying | rewriting of dictation; developing study skills; responding to literature |

The remainder of this book provides detailed suggestions for managing instruction for students at each stage. The program features outlined in Table 1-2 are elaborated. We suggest numerous designs for oral language activities, dictation sessions, and reinforcement activities. Word recognition activities and ways to teach writing are also included in separate chapters. Finally, we provide an example of a successful modification of our basic plan to illustrate the flexibility of the approach.

Our suggested lessons and activities throughout may need to be modified to suit the ages and interests of a particular group. The basic *procedures* we outline for each stage are suitable for students of any age, as we have repeatedly confirmed in our own teaching and as our colleagues have found in their classes. It is the *content* of discussions/dictation that will vary depending on student age. A topic that interests a seven-year-old will not necessarily engage an adult although their levels of English competency require the same instructional procedures. The way directions are given and the way students are handled will also, of course, vary with student age. We stress these points because some educators believe that teaching procedures must be basically different for children and adults. We have found that this is not so. It is the level of oral skills that should determine lesson procedures, not the age of the student.

# REFERENCES

Asher, J. J. *Learning Another Language Through Actions.* Los Gatos, CA: Sky Oaks Productions, 1977.

Brown, H.D. "The Seventies: Learning to Ask the Right Questions." *Language Learning,* June, 1979, *29,* v-vi.

Brown, R. *A First Language: The Early Stages.* Cambridge: Harvard University Press, 1973.

Brown, R., and Hanlon, C. "Derivational Complexity and Order of Acquisition." in Hayes, J., Ed. *Cognition and the Development of Language.* New York: J. Wiley, 1970, 11-53.

Hall, G. E., and Loucks, S. F. "A Developmental Model for Determining Whether the Treatment is Actually Implemented." *American Educational Research Journal 14, Summer, 1977, 14,* 263-76.

Hall, G. E., Loucks, S. F., Rutherford, W. L., and Newlove, B. W. "Levels of Use of the Innovation: A Framework for Analyzing Innovation Adoption." *Journal of Teacher Education,* Spring, 1975, *26,* 52-56.

Krashen, S. D. *Second Language Acquisition.* Oxford: The Pergamon Press, 1981.

Krashen, S. D., and Terrell, T. D. *The Natural Approach.* San Francisco: The Alemany Press, 1983.

La Puma, L. *How Language is Learned: First and Second Language Acquisition.* Unpublished M.A. thesis, University of California at Santa Barbara, 1981.

Nelson, K. *Structure and Strategy in Learning to Talk.* Monographs of the Society for Research in Child Development, Serial No. 149 1-2, 1973, *38,* 1-137.

# Chapter 2

# The Stage 1 Student

Stage 1 students have virtually no oral English ability and most typically are recent arrivals to the U.S. as part of an immigrant family whose other members also have limited abilities with English. Many of these learners come to school timid and frightened by the unfamiliar surroundings and expectations. They are confronted with strange experiences and incomprehensible people. Frequently, they are unable to communicate their most basic needs and concerns because no one understands their language. Besides facing a language barrier, they are simultaneously adjusting to a new home, a new culture, a new life style, and perhaps the need to obtain employment and support a family. The transition is stressful, even overwhelming. Some students may not easily catch on to classroom routines and demands and may be either excessively withdrawn or openly belligerent in their attempts to adjust.

Besides having limitations with general English language skills, the Stage 1 student may also lack other relevant knowledge or experience. Many lack familiarity with any written language, perhaps being too young to have learned to read and write their native language or, as older students, having not attended school nor achieved basic literacy in their homeland. Some may not even fully realize that the little black marks on the page represent words that are used orally. Students whose oral language does not have a written counterpart may have an especially difficult time acquiring the concept of reading words in print. Others may have had experiences with their own written language (being read to or recognizing signs and labels) but have not learned to read their native language.

These students need the care and concern of sensitive and understanding teachers. They also need an instructional program that will, as a first step, help them learn to understand and speak English. Even if teachers or classmates do speak their language, these students must eventually learn to master the basics of the English language if they are to participate fully in American society. Relying continually on their native language may make some aspects of their adjustment easier but will only delay their opportunities for communicating with fellow students and other members of the society that is now their home.

## ORAL LANGUAGE AND READING

Stage 1 students vividly demonstrate the important role of oral language experience in learning to read. The average English-speaking kindergartner has had several years of total immersion in oral language before attempting to learn basic reading skills. The Stage 1 ESL student, whether a six-year-old, a teenager, or an adult, has an almost complete lack of background with oral English. Placing Stage 1 students immediately in a reading program, no matter how well designed, usually results in frustration for both student and teacher. They must first acquire sufficient background in *oral* English to feel comfortable with the vocabulary and structures. These students simply must not be expected to learn to recognize English words, master English phonics, read English-language readers, or in other ways undergo typical reading instruction as if they were simply English-speaking non-readers. LEA for Stage 1 students requires initial emphasis on oral language. Reading instruction begins only after the student has gained confidence in using oral English.

## PROCEDURES FOR STAGE 1 STUDENTS

### Oral Language Activities

It makes sense to begin a Stage 1 student's language program with English words and sentences that will be immediately useful. The sooner these learners are able to make themselves understood and understand those around them, the sooner they will feel comfortable in their new environment and be ready to profit from school. Students need to learn to carry on conversations, make requests, respond to directions, ask and answer questions, and in other ways learn the necessary vocabulary to survive. Individual and small group activities should introduce vocabulary and common language structures. The emphasis should be on teaching vocabulary and expressions that are directly related to the student's daily life, to the people, objects, and events encountered in school and at home. "Basic" vocabulary will vary from one Stage 1 student to another, depending on age, particular surroundings, and unique concerns. Above all, the student must be provided with an environment rich in both oral and written English language experiences and given the freedom to chance mistakes without fear of penalty.

Usually English-speaking classmates will be willing to help the Stage 1 student acquire oral English skills. In fact, fellow students are often the best teachers because of their eagerness to make a new friend. Classmates also can devote more time than the teacher in one-to-one conversation with a student. Willing native English speakers should thus be given many opportunities to interact with the Stage 1 student. Informal conversations in the lunchroom or on school grounds, as well as in the classroom, will often be as helpful to the ESL learner as carefully planned, teacher directed activities. If students are assigned to a special ESL class, it might take some extra planning to arrange activities with English-speaking peers. ESL students might be scheduled into regular classrooms for films or other special events, or English-speaking students might be invited regularly to visit the ESL classroom to talk with the students.

A unit is outlined here to illustrate how a combination of teacher direction and classmate help can be used to teach a Stage 1 student to name common objects found in the classroom. This plan can serve as a model for instructional units to meet any number of oral language objectives. The unit is also designed to prepare students for eventual reading instruction.

*Instructional Unit:* Naming Objects
*Objective:* Student will be able to name and describe at least fifteen\* objects in the classroom.
*Length of unit:* One week

## Day 1

*Activity 1*

Prepare fifteen cards with mounted or drawn pictures of objects that can be found in the classroom (desk, chair, book, etc.). Label the cards clearly with the most common English word for each object and tell the student that this is the way the word _____ is written in English. The intent is not to teach recognition of the written words but rather to get the student used to seeing English words in print. Seeing the labels, the student can acquire the concept of a written language in a natural manner, just as native English speakers often acquire the concept of reading through noting signs and labels around them. Figure 2-A illustrates one of these word cards.

---

\*This number is not magic. It may be reduced if necessary for a particular student. However, since classroom object words have high utility, this number will not be unreasonable for most students.

Figure 2-A

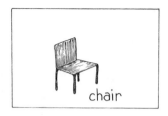

Show five cards to the student, one at at time, saying the name of each object as the card is presented. Show and name each card at least twice. Then have the student repeat the names (give help as needed). Go through the cards several times until the student seems to have learned the names.

Introduce the question "What is this?" and the reply "This is a(n) _____." Show each of the cards again a few times, in each instance repeating the question and having the student give the proper reply. Give whatever help is needed by saying the object names and/or the reply with the student. Although this instruction uses simple patterned questions and responses, these should not be presented in a rigid, stilted way. Intonation, stress, and facial expressions should be natural and realistic so that the student is engaged in a real conversation while learning to use these common words and patterns.

After the first five cards have been introduced in this manner, go through the next set of five cards and then the last set in the same way.

*Activity 2*

Read or tell a simple story to the student. Choose or compose a story that includes one or more of the object names used in Activity 1 so the student will have a chance to recognize the recently learned words. Use pictures or other visual aids (puppets, models, objects, etc.) to help the student follow the story line. This activity reinforces learning of object names and also exposes the student to additional oral English.

## Day 2

*Activity 1*

Review learning by presenting the fifteen cards, one at a time. Again ask "What is this?" and help the student answer "This is a(n) _____" for each.

*Activity 2*

Walk around the room with the student, asking "What is this?" when coming to each of the objects represented in the pictures. Help the student answer when necessary. An English-speaking classmate may also be asked to do this with the Stage 1 student.

## Day 3

*Activity 1*

Form a group of several learners, including the Stage 1 student. Hand out bingo cards on which have been placed drawings or pictures of the fifteen objects in the original picture set, labeled with their English names. Call out the names of the objects and have students place markers on the proper illustrations on their cards. Be sure to go slowly enough to allow the ESL student to make correct decisions. (Some ESL students may need to review the original card set again before playing this game.)

*Activity 2*

Pair the Stage 1 student with an English-speaking classmate. Have them walk around the room and name the key objects as they come to them as in Activity 2 for Day 2. The English-speaking student may also introduce the names of a few more objects in this manner if the Stage 1 student seems ready to learn more object names at this time.

## Day 4

*Activity 1*

Using the original picture cards, introduce the Stage 1 student to the colors and/or size of the objects. For example, hold up a card and say "This is a book. This is a *red* book." Other aids may be necessary to clarify the meaning of these descriptive words. For instance, gestures may be used to indicate size, or other, similarly colored objects may be indicated to illustrate color concepts. Have the student respond to the basic "What is this?" question with the expanded statements.

*Activity 2*

Read aloud or tell another simple story. Again choose or compose a story that includes some of the words that have been introduced to this point. Use visual aids to help the student follow events in the story.

## Day 5

*Activity 1*

Review the fifteen objects with the student. Go through the picture cards one at a time,having the student name each object by saying "This is a(n) _____." Then have the student name the real objects in the room the same way. Help the student use the descriptive words learned the day before. ("This is a door. This is a *brown* door.") A classmate might be asked to lead this review. Interaction with another person is the most desirable form of review. However, additional review may be provided by preparing object cards to be used with a Language Master or Voxcom.

*Activity 2*

Read aloud or tell another story to the student, or have a classmate do this. Again choose a story that includes a few of the words learned during the week, and use visual aids to illustrate.

These activities can be used with individuals, or several Stage 1 students may be grouped together for the various tasks. Repetition from day to day is accomplished in a meaningful and pleasant context, helping to cement learning of key words and phrases. The stories read aloud or told reinforce some of the new vocabulary as well as introduce additional words, language structures, and the general sense of English. Learning will be reinforced as students hear and use the same words and patterns in informal situations during the day.

This unit is only one example of how Stage 1 students can begin to acquire an oral English vocabulary. Other instructional units may be set up, using the same principles of meaningful repetition, real world situations, and focus on language elements of immediate necessity. Additional topics are suggested here. In some of these activities it is advisable to allow the student to listen to the models of English without being forced to respond or participate.

1. *Conversations.* Ask English-speaking classmates to help act out various typical conversations for the Stage 1 student to observe and then join. Use pictures or real objects when possible to illustrate key concepts. Gestures and facial expressions may also help to illustrate meaning in some situations. For example, plan structured conversations to introduce:

   a. greetings (Good morning. Hello.)
   b. common inquiries (How are you? What time is it?)
   c. common topics of conversation (lunch table talk about food, discussion of the weather, talk about sporting events.)

2. *Language in typical social situations.* Have English-speaking students act out situations which illustrate participation in various social events. The Stage 1 student may observe and join in when ready. For example,

   a. ordering a meal in a restaurant (How much is this? I would like to have a hamburger, please. This is "to go.")
   b. dealing with a bus driver (I want to go to _____. How much is the fare? Please take me to _____.)
   c. attending recreational events (How much is a ticket? Can you help me find my seat?)

3. *Using survival words and symbols.* Have English-speaking students act out situations stressing attention to various symbols that are necessary to basic survival and comfort both in the school and in the larger community. Signs and props may be used to illustrate. The Stage 1 student may observe and join in when ready. For example, build situations involving:

*Survival/comfort in society*

a. Walk/Don't Walk signals
b. Stop Signs
c. Danger! and other warning signs
d. Out of Order notices
e. Emergency Exit information
f. fire alarms
g. poison warnings
h. Men/Women signs
i. police station signs
j. hospital emergency room situations

*Survival/comfort in school*

a. requests to teachers (May I get a drink of water? May I go to the bathroom?)
b. activities involving different school areas (programs in the auditorium, cafeteria regulations, gymnasium/playground rules and customs)
c. requests for help from different school personnel (need for the nurse's office, conference with a counselor, meeting with an administrator, interaction with the librarian)
d. following teacher directions (Sit down. Turn in your paper. Close your books. Come over here.)

Besides specially planned instructional units, activity centers could be set up in the room to provide independent oral language practice. These centers may be used individually by Stage 1 students, or the students may be paired with one another or English-speaking classmates for some of the activities. Activity centers may include such things as:

a. puppets for extemporaneous puppet shows or informal conversations with classmates
b. telephones for practice conversations emphasizing greetings and other high-use statements
c. taped stories with accompanying read-along books
d. sound films or filmstrips
e. collections of objects and pictures for learning object names

Commercial programs are available for teaching many necessary and immediately useful English words and language structures. We list here a few of these oral language programs that have been designed for these purposes. They may be used for planning additional lessons for Stage 1 students or may provide ideas as to which language elements to emphasize. Although most are intended for use with young students (grades K-3), the activities and methods may be adapted for use with older students as well.

Asher, James J. *Learning Another Language Through Actions.* Los

Gatos, CA: Sky Oaks Production, 1977.

Gonzales-Mena, Janet. *English Experiences*. Silver Spring, MD: Institute for Modern Languages, 1975.

Lancaster, Louise. *Introducing English*. Hopewell, NJ: Houghton Mifflin, 1975.

McCallum, George P. *101 Word Games: For Students of English as a Second or Foreign Language*. New York: Oxford University Press, 1980.

Mellgren, Lars and Walker, Michael. *Yes! Young English Series, Book A*. Reading, MA: Addison Wesley, 1977.

Olshar, Laura and Wilson, Robert. *Beginning Fluency in English as a New Language*. Los Angeles: Bowmar, 1967.

As the Stage 1 student makes progress learning English, lessons and activities may be extended to include a greater variety of tasks designed to increase familiarity with oral English. Whenever possible, the student should be encouraged to help select topics for lessons. A student who is worried about an upcoming trip to the doctor, for example, will be far more interested in learning words such as *doctor, nurse, medicine,* and *shot* than the names of months or the days of the week.

As students' vocabularies expand, wordless picture books are particularly valuable for extending language learning. These materials have easily recognizable stories or themes which appeal to students of all ages. Students can "read" and discuss them with the teacher and other students. Oral language is developed while the student has a successful experience with books. Suitable wordless books include:

Books which tell a story:

Alexander, Martha. *Bobo's Dream*. New York: Dial Press, 1970.

Ardizzone, Ed. *The Wrong Side of the Bed*. New York: Doubleday, 1970.

Carle, Eric. *Do You Want To Be a Friend?* New York: Thomas Crowell, 1971.

Carroll, Ruth. *What Whiskers Did*. New York: Henry Walck, 1965.

———— and Carroll, Latrobe. *The Christmas Kitten*. New York: Henry Walck, 1970.

Fromm, Lila. *Muffel and Plums*. New York: Macmillan, 1973.

Goodall, John. *Creepy Castle*. New York: Atheneum, 1977.

————. *The Ballooning Adventures of Paddy Pork*. New York: Harcourt, Brace, Jovanovich, 1969

————. *The Surprise Picnic*. New York: Atheneum, 1977.

Krahn, Fernando. *April Fools*. New York: E.P. Dutton, 1974.

————. *The Mystery of the Giant Footprints.* New York: E.P. Dutton, 1977.

————. *Who's Seen the Scissors?* New York: E.P. Dutton, 1975.

Mayer, Mercer. *A Boy, A Dog, and A Frog.* New York: Dial Press, 1967.

————. *A Boy, A Dog, A Frog, and A Friend.* New York: Dial Press, 1971.

————. *Ah-Choo.* New York: Dial Press, 1976.

————. *Frog Goes to Dinner.* New York: Dial Press, 1974.

————. *Frog On His Own.* New York: Dial Press, 1973.

————. *Frog, Where Are You?* New York: Dial Press, 1969.

————. *Hiccup.* New York: Dial Press, 1976.

————. *One Frog Too Many.* New York: Dial Press, 1975.

————. *The Great Cat Chase.* New York: Dial Press, 1974.

Books which develop a theme or event:

Emberley, Ed. *A Birthday Wish.* Boston: Little, Brown, 1977.

Hogrogian, Nonny. *Apples.* New York: Macmillan, 1972.

Kent, Jack. *The Egg Book.* New York: Macmillan, 1975.

Mari, Iela and Mari, Enzo. *The Apple and the Moth.* New York: Pantheon, 1970.

————. *The Chicken and the Egg.* New York: Pantheon, 1970.

Shimin, Symeon. *A Special Birthday.* New York: McGraw-Hill, 1976.

McTrusty, Ron. *Dandelion Year.* New York: Hawey House, 1975.

Books which present an abstract concept:

Anno, Mitsuma. *Topsie Turvies.* New York: Weatherhill, 1972.

Hoban, Tana. *Look Again!* New York: Macmillan, 1971.

Hutchins, Pat. *Changes, Changes.* New York: Macmillan, 1971.

Lisker, Sonia. *Lost.* New York: Harcourt, Brace, Jovanovich, 1975.

Turkle, Brinton. *Deep in the Forest.* New York: E.P. Dutton, 1976.

Ungerer, Toni. *One, Two, Where's My Shoe.* New York: Harper & Row, 1964.

————. *Snail, Where Are You?* New York: Harper & Row, 1962

Depending on age, ability, and psychological readiness, the Stage 1 student will take several weeks, several months, or most of a school year to acquire enough facility with English to begin a program of reading instruction. Generally, Stage 1 students are ready for reading instruction when they begin to recognize written English words on the oral language lesson cards or when they try to identify words in books or signs in their environment. At this point students will usually be able to read one or two highly meaningful words, such as their names or words like *stop, walk,* or *exit.* There is no specific criterion for deciding when the student is ready, though. The best way is to begin reading instruction when the student seems ready by showing an interest in printed English. If the student makes progress, instruction may be continued; if it seems too frustrating, oral language training should be emphasized until the student seems better able to profit from reading activities. As students gradually acquire the concept of how written language works, they will also begin to realize that print is less than talk written down since it lacks the cues provided in oral communication by gestures, facial expression, pauses, and intonation. It is important that the student not be overwhelmed by these differences. Continued experience with meaningful written English associated with real life situations will help stress that reading is as valuable a form of communication as speaking.

## *Reading Activities*

The same basic principles are used to introduce reading activities as are used for developing oral language. The emphasis is on acquiring a reading vocabulary that is personally meaningful and immediately useful. "Basic" reading vocabulary will vary from one student to another since each student differs in terms of interests, maturity, and experience background. Language experience procedures capitalize on these differences, allowing the student to begin to read materials that match unique, personal interests.

The first phase in learning to read involves the use of a "key vocabulary,"** selected by the student because the words are familiar, interesting, or useful. In most key vocabulary approaches the student is given totally free choice in selecting words to be learned. Structured choice is frequently more desirable for the Stage 1 student. Since oral language lessons are continuing, the student should be encouraged to choose words from these activities as a basis for reading instruction. If the student has had a voice in selecting the topic for the oral language activity, the words available for choice will still be highly significant. These are the steps to follow:

1. Conduct an informal conversation with the student on a topic that will generate interest. Talk about something personally meaningful

---

**These procedures are adapted from several "key vocabulary" sources, notably Ashton-Warner (1963) and Veatch, et al. (1979).

and relevant to the student, for example, a favorite activity, recent family pursuits, or special events in which the student is involved. The point of the conversation is to elicit as many English words on the topic as possible. Open-ended questions encourage talk and elaboration of descriptions and explanations.

2. After conversing for several minutes, tell the student to choose some words (no more than five) from the conversation. Explain that together you will be *reading* these words and so they should be words the student really wants to learn.

3. Print each chosen word on a 3x5 card. Read the words several times with the student.

4. Have the student copy the words into the appropriate places in a personal picture dictionary and illustrate each word. The word should always be placed on the left side of the page and the drawing or cut-out picture on the right so that the illustrations can be folded under and the student can read the words without the picture cues in review activities. The 3x5 card should be retained in a deck of word cards.

5. Direct the student to a variety of other materials (books, newspapers, magazines) to search for the chosen words. Have the student underline, circle, or cut out these words and then read them aloud. This can also be done as a small group, or pairs, activity.

In this way oral language development and learning to read are profitably combined in the same instructional unit. A sample unit is outlined here to illustrate how that combination may work. The topics for these units should always be relevant to the student's daily life.

> *Instructional Unit:* A Trip to the Grocery Store
> *Objectives:* Student will be able to use orally many words related to the topic
> Student will be able to read up to five words related to the topic
> *Length of unit:* One week

### Day 1

*Activity 1*

Discuss the topic, the grocery store, with the student. List several of the most significant words used in the discussion on a large sheet of newsprint or the chalkboard. Words used might include: meat, eggs, cans, clerk, money.

*Activity 2*

Have the student select several words (no more than five) to learn to read. Print each of the chosen words on its own 3x5 card. Read each word card several times with the student.

*Activity 3*
Have the student copy each word in a picture dictionary and illustrate with a drawing or cut out picture.

## Day 2

*Activity 1*
Briefly review the previous day's discussion. Reread the word cards with the student, referring to the picture dictionary for any forgotten words.

*Activity 2*
Have the student role play the trip to the store with another student.

## Day 3

*Activity 1*
Review the word cards with the student. Any words which are not instantly recognized should be discarded at this time. One or two new words may be put on cards and added to the deck if the student wishes, following the same procedure as Day 1.

*Activity 2*
Read the student a simple story that contains many of the chosen words. If an appropriate story is not available, it is easy enough to write one to use. A teacher written story can be made personal by using the student's name and referring to the student's favorite foods.

*Activity 3*
Have the student search for and underline the chosen words in a copy of the story just read aloud. (If it is not desirable to mark the original copy, use a plastic overlay and a wax pencil.)

## Day 4

*Activity 1*
Review any new word cards added the previous day.

*Activity 2*
From a collection of assorted pictures have the student select ones which correctly depict the chosen words.

## Day 5

*Activity 1*
Review any new word cards added the third day, *discarding* those that are not remembered.

*Activity 2*

Discuss the ways in which a trip to the grocery store is similar to and different from a trip to a gas station, a park, or other places familiar to the student.

*Activity 3*

Have the student use the word card deck to play "Concentration" with another student. Blank "wild cards" should be added to the deck and cards added to provide duplicates of the original words. The words matched must also be read correctly for players to keep pairs.

In subsequent lessons, use the word cards to review all the chosen words from the preceding two or three days' work as well as several words chosen at random from earlier lessons. If the student fails to identify a word correctly two days in a row, remove that word from the deck. It is important that the card deck provide an accurate picture for both the teacher and the student of the student's increasing ability to read English words. If words are truly significant to the student they will reappear and be chosen again in future lessons. The picture dictionary will keep all words on file. This will become a self-teaching aid for later reading activities. The word card deck and the picture dictionary should be used in a variety of practice activities. (The size of the word deck is not crucial. Even very small decks of two or three cards can give students good practice identifying words and making decisions about word categories.) Here are some sample activities:

1. *Word Card Activities*
   a. Have two or more students select a category such as food, colors, or sports. Have them search their card decks for words which fit that category and compare their choices with each other.
   b. Discuss a new word with students such as "hungry." Have them select word cards which make them think of "hungry."
   c. Have an English-speaking student ask simple questions like "Do you have a _____ (toy, pet, color, etc.)?" The ESL student selects an appropriate answer card from the deck.
   d. Have two students working together take turns selecting a word and challenging the other to find a matching or opposite word.
   e. Have students play a card game such as "Old Maid" by matching cards with the same first letter.

2. *Picture Dictionary Activities*
   a. Have students fold the pages in their picture dictionaries so

that only the words are visible. Have them take turns selecting
a page from their dictionaries and reading the words aloud.
Students may earn points for each word read correctly.

b. Fold pages in picture dictionaries so only words are visible.
Have students draw or select pictures which match the words,
then open the page and check choices. Where pictures differ,
e.g., two different breeds to illustrate *dog*, discuss why both
pictures are appropriate.

c. Have students fold the pages in their picture dictionaries so
that only the pictures are visible and select cards from their
word decks to label the pictures. The page may then be opened
to check choices.

d. Have two or more students trade dictionaries. Fold pages so
only illustrations are visible and have students select words
from their card decks to label pictures. When the chosen word
differs from the dictionary owner's word, have students decide
why both labels are/are not appropriate.

Other useful practice activities may be adapted from several sources. For
additional ideas we particularly recommend Spache (1976) and Burns and
Roe (1979).

## TRANSITION TO STAGE 2

As soon as the student has acquired a reading vocabulary of two or
three dozen English words, it is possible to move to the dictation of
simple sentences. This can involve the use of pattern stories, stories in
which certain language structures are repeated throughout. These stories
build additional aural/oral skills and make the process of dictating simple
English sentences relatively easy.

After listening to and discussing a pattern story, the student should
dictate several sentences following the introduced pattern. The student
may then illustrate the transcribed statements, a task which is enjoyable
and which reinforces comprehension of the written statements as they are
reread. If each statement is recorded and illustrated on a separate page,
these dictated pattern stories can be simply bound into small books and
read with teacher help. Individual words from the stories may also be
placed on word cards, to be added to the student's word deck.

Figure 2-B illustrates a portion of a pattern story composed and
dictated by a seven-year-old Laotian girl. The stimulus was the book by
Bill Martin, Jr., *When It Rains, It Rains* (New York: Holt, Rinehart and
Winston, 1971). After listening to and discussing the story, Kazoua
followed the basic pattern and composed a delightful collection of
statements and illustrations that was bound and "published" by her

teacher.***

Figure 2-B

When I swim,
   I swim.

When I sleep, I sleep.

When I jump,
   I jump.

When I'm a queen,
   I'm a queen.

When I go to the
        mountains,
   I go to the mountains.

***Millie Farnum, Reading Specialist, Ellwood School, Goleta, CA.

Listening to a pattern story, such as *When It Rains, It Rains,* and then dictating an imitative story provides an excellent way of integrating oral language and reading. However, these activities do not have to be limited to the patterns in published books. Pattern stories or books may be developed easily by having the student describe an object or event by repeating any desired sentence form. For example, "Dogs like to bark" may be used as the basis of a story which might include variations such as:

> Dogs like to bark.
>
> Dogs like to play.
>
> Dogs like to chew bones.
>
> Dogs like to sleep.

Figure 2-C illustrates a simple sentence pattern which served as the basis for one Stage 1 student's dictation and drawing.

Figure 2-C

In another very successful activity, Kazoua's teacher used a story written by a native English-speaking student, Nancy, to provide a more complex pattern.

### Nancy's story

Once upon a time there was a little girl. Her name was Sue. She wanted a horse. When her birthday came she got a horse. She loved her horse. She named her horse Sunny. Now, Sunny wasn't a pony. She was a horse. She loved Sue.

### Kazoua's story

Once upon a time there was a little girl. Her name was Meesy. She wanted a cat. When her birthday came she got a cat. She loved her cat. She named her cat Kitten. Now, Kitten wasn't a dog. She was a cat. Meesy loved her cat.

As confidence grows, students are sometimes able to use a series of patterns to produce a longer account. Carline's story illustrates the result of combining several patterns for dictation.

### Carline's story

Once upon a time there was a woman. Her name was Leila. She wanted a little rabbit. When Christmas came Leila got her rabbit. He was a white rabbit with a bushy tail. She needs food for the rabbit. The rabbit's name was Bushy Tail. She loved to play with Bushy Tail.

One day Bushy Tail had a baby. The baby's name was Little Bushy Tail. Her mom named her Little Bushy Tail because she looked just like her.

Little Bushy Tail had a friend. Her friend's name was Jana. She was a rabbit too. They liked to laugh and play. Their favorite game was Hide and Go Seek.

Once Little Bushy Tail had a birthday. She wanted a pony. She got a pony. Little Bushy Tail loved her pony. Her pony's name was Cutie. The pony was a girl.

Books useful for pattern story dictation include:

DeLage, Ida. *Hello, Come In.* New Canaan, CT: Garrard, 1971.

Domanska, Janina. *Spring Is.* New York: Greenwillow, 1976.

Eastman, P.D. *Go, Dog. Go!* New York: Random House, 1961.

Krauss, Ruth. *A Hole is to Dig.* New York: Harper & Row, 1952.

McCracken, Robert A., and McCracken, Marlene J.
*Tiger Cub Readers*. San Rafael, CA: Leswing Press, 1973.
Selected titles:
*One Pig, Two Pigs*
*The End. . .*
*The Farmer and the Skunk*
*The Farmer Had a Pig*
*What Can You Do?*
*What Can You Hear?*
*What Can You See?*
*What Do You Do?*
*What is This?*
*Where Do You Live?*

Martin, Bill Jr., *Instant Readers*. New York: Holt, Rinehart & Winston, 1971. Selected titles:

LEVEL I

*Brown Bear, Brown Bear, What Do You See?*
*When It Rains, It Rains*
*The Haunted House*
*Silly Goose and the Holidays*
*I Went to the Market*
*The Wizard*
*Monday, Monday, I Like Monday*
*Up and Down the Escalator*

LEVEL II

*King of the Mountain*
*The Longest Journey in the World*
*Whistle, Mary, Whistle*
*A Spooky Story*
*City Song*

LEVEL III

*My Days Are Made of Butterflies*
*The Turning of the Year*
*I Paint the Joy of a Flower*
*Ten Little Squirrels*

Scheer, Julian. *Upside Down Day*. New York: Holiday House, 1968.

Seuss, Dr. *One Fish, Two Fish, Red Fish, Blue Fish*. New York: Random House, 1960.

_____ . *Green Eggs and Ham*. New York: Random House, 1960.

Zolotow, Charlotte. *Summer Is . . .* New York: Abelard-Schuman, 1967.

Pattern stories are much like a beginning swimmer's water wings. They provide a useful means for moving learning forward but are not an end in themselves any more than staying afloat with water wings is equivalent to swimming across the pool unaided. As soon as students are able to dictate sentences in English with ease, dictation should move to Stage 2 procedures.

## SUMMARY

At Stage 1, student oral language skills are developed through a variety of meaningful, real life activities. When the student is ready, reading instruction is begun with use of a modified "key vocabulary" approach. Eventually the student begins dictating statements, based on pattern stories. Various reinforcement activities build oral language ability and help students begin to learn to process written English.

## REFERENCES

Ashton-Warner, S. *Teacher*. New York: Simon and Schuster, 1963.

Burns, P. C., and Roe, B. D. *Reading Activities for Today's Elementary Schools*. Chicago: Rand McNally, 1979.

Spache, E. *Reading Activities for Child Involvement*. Boston: Allyn and Bacon, 1976.

Veatch, J., Sawicki, F., Elliot, G., Flake, E., and Blakey, J. *Key Words to Reading: The Language Experience Approach Begins*. Columbus: Charles Merrill, 1979.

# Chapter 3

# The Stage 2 Student

The second and most typical ESL student is the Stage 2 student, one with some English language skills and some familiarity with a written language, either a native language or English. As with Stage 1 students, Stage 2 students may be children, adolescents, or adults. This student is able to conduct simple conversations in English and is making good progress toward understanding spoken English. Also, the student will have had some exposure to reading instruction, either in the native language or in English. Stage 1 students become Stage 2 students when they have made good progress with typical Stage 1 oral language and reading activities. These students still need considerable practice with English as an oral language, but they already understand that written words are a code for language used orally. They are ready for a more complete reading program in English as long as the lessons are meaningful and non-threatening.

## PROCEDURES FOR STAGE 2 STUDENTS

A step-by-step plan for developing reading skills may be used with the Stage 2 student, incorporating another variation of the Language Experience Approach. The basic principles of this plan are similar to those used when working with the Stage 1 student. First, teacher and student construct the basic reading material through student dictation. Comprehension of written English is thus accomplished with ease since the student only reads self-generated, meaningful statements. Second, sight vocabulary is developed by giving the student many carefully planned contacts with the familiar words of the dictated story. There is greater emphasis on word learning activities at Stage 2 than there is at Stage 1. Activities are made gradually more challenging as the lessons proceed, but the tasks are designed to allow the student to learn at a comfortable rate. Third, the teacher is ever supportive, accepting the student's English statements and adjusting the activities and schedule to promote success. Finally, while developing reading skills, the teacher has many opportunities to assess oral language needs in order to plan continuing oral English lessons.

## *Basic Teaching Plan*

This plan is organized into daily instructional units. It can be adapted for use in a regular classroom, a special ESL classroom, or a tutorial setting. We have outlined the basic steps to conform to a five-day sequence of lessons. Some students may need longer to complete this sequence; others may be able to do it in less time.

### Day 1

*Step 1: Conducting the discussion*

To develop the basis for a dictated story, encourage the student to discuss any topic of significant, personal interest. (Appropriate stimulus topics are reviewed on page 40.) Conduct the discussion to draw out the student's ideas, expressed in the student's own way. The oral English practice at this point is valuable in its own right; the conversation should be a supportive and pleasant exchange to encourage fluency and confidence. Avoid making corrections in English usage at this time, but supply words as needed. Keep questions open-ended to get the student to describe, explain, or react to the stimulus.

Discussions will vary in length, depending on the age, attention, and ideas of the learner. Generally, once the student has made several observations, enabling an account to be constructed, it is time to begin dictation.

*Step 2: Taking dictation*

The first few times dictation is taken, briefly explain the procedure to the student. Some workable directions are:

> You have told me some interesting things about _____ .
> Now it is time to write down some of your ideas. How shall
> we begin your story?

If the student is uncertain how to begin, prompt by suggesting one of the student's previous statements as a starter. One such exchange went like this:

> Teacher: Remember, you told me how you helped your
> brother at home yesterday. You said, "I help my brother
> work on the car." Let's start with that (writing down the
> statement). Tell me what happened then.

Student: My brother was changing oil.

Teacher: Good. We'll put that down next. Go on.

While the learner dictates the account, record the story *exactly as the student gives it* without making corrections in English usage or idea organization. The goal is to construct an account that reflects the learner's language, not one that is perfectly stated or organized from the start. The main purpose of this step is preparation for acquiring English language *reading* skills. The student will attempt to read the material the way he or she originally stated it. If changes are made, the student can easily become confused. Furthermore, it is extremely important that instruction not damage the student's still fragile self concept as an English speaker. Accepting any English statements made during dictation will help to build self confidence.

The length of dictation will vary from one student to another or, for one learner, from one occasion to another. Three or four statements will make a good dictated account, or longer stories can be taken. The dictation should be long enough to provide a variety of words and sentences but not so long as to be frustrating to work with later. After working with a student for a few lessons, it will be easier to judge suitable length.

Immediately after the dictation is completed, read the account aloud to the student and ask for any changes or additions. Make modifications accordingly. Of course, the student may not wish to change or add anything; alterations at this point are allowable but not necessary. Then read the story several times with the student. The first two steps are now complete, and the student can go on to another activity while preparations are made for further instruction.

*Step 3: Preparing for instruction*

To prepare for Day 2 instruction, type or print two copies of the story, using double or triple spacing for visual ease and keeping the learner's statements exactly as dictated. On a separate paper, make notes of usage and vocabulary difficulties that occurred in the dictation. A prepared dictated story, based on discussion of a picture of a boy and a frog, and the accompanying teacher notes in Figure 3-A illustrate this step.

Figure 3-A                    ***Dictated story***

**Frog**

He is look the frog. He is sit down in the desk. This day is night. He is asleep.

***Assessment of needs***

1. use of the *ing* ending
2. use of the preposition *at*
3. use of the pronoun *it* to replace the awkward "this day"

At this point there are two different goals: helping the student learn to read some of the words in this dictated story and planning English language activities to remedy any problems noted.

The student begins to learn words from the story through a cycle of activities, similar to the procedures often used to help English-speaking remedial readers.* The student is not expected to learn *all* of the words in the story; the cycle is designed for accommodation to the student's own rate of learning.

## Day 2

*Step 1: Silent reading*

Give the student one copy of the dictated story to read silently. If the student seems to have difficulty, read the story aloud with the student as on Day 1. After the first reading, the student should reread the story and underline all known words. Underlining *known* words gives the activity a positive emphasis that enhances the student's self esteem.

Self assessment is often difficult for some students. Some may underestimate what they know and underline only a few words because they may be very cautious or even afraid of being criticized if they later forget a word. Others may overestimate what they know and will underline almost every word because they may be overconfident or may believe they are expected to know everything right from the start. Some students may just not understand what they are to do so that their underlining will not reflect what they actually know. After several stories and support from the encouraging teacher, most students will learn to be reasonably accurate in their self appraisals. The student who learns to make a realistic self assessment will benefit from the active involvement in learning and the pride that comes from seeing real growth as time goes on.

*Step 2: Oral reading*

Once the student has read the story silently, have him or her read it aloud. If the student hesitates or seems confused about a word, supply that word to maintain the flow of the story. Use the second copy of the story to keep a record of the oral reading, marking words with which the student has difficulty, noting pronunciation problems, and marking additions or omissions the student makes. Do this recording openly. If the student asks about the marking, matter-of-factly say that this is done to decide how best to help the student. Later, compare this record with the student's self assessment, indicated by the words underlined on the

*This adaptation originated with Dr. Russell G. Stauffer when he was Director of The Reading-Study Center, University of Delaware, Newark, DE. It is also described in Stauffer, et al. (1978) and in Nessel and Jones (1980).

student's copy, to get an idea of the student's self knowledge and self confidence.

## Step 3: Sequential List

This step begins preparing the student to identify story words in other materials, that is, outside the context of the familiar story. Provide the student with a Sequential List, a list of all the story words in the same order in which they appeared in the story. Figure 3-B illustrates a Sequential List made from the story "Frog."

*Figure 3-B* **Sequential List**

**Frog**

| He | down | He |
|------|-------|--------|
| is | in | is |
| look | the | asleep |
| the | desk | |
| frog | This | |
| He | day | |
| is | is | |
| sit | night | |

While the words are presented in the order in which they occurred in the story (a meaningful context), the altered visual arrangement changes the familiar context somewhat and makes the task slightly more challenging. Ask the student to read the list aloud, and again keep a record of word identification on a second copy of the list. This record will help in analyzing difficulties with particular words and planning needed word recognition instruction. Place a check beside each word the student identifies easily and without help. Figure 3-C illustrates the analysis made during the reading of the Sequential List from "Frog."

*Figure 3-C* **Sequential List: Analysis of Oral Reading**

**Frog** _____ √ _____

| He | √ | down | DK | He | √ |
|------|------|-------|------|--------|------|
| is | √ | in | DK | is | √ |
| look | lɪk | the | √ | asleep | √ |
| the | √ | desk | dɑsk | | |
| frog | √ | This | DK | | |
| He | √ | day | √ | | |
| is | √ | is | √ | | |
| sit | sat | night | √ | | |

*DK* = doesn't know

This activity completes the lesson for this second day. With some students it may be desirable to repeat the three steps the following day before proceeding to the more difficult Day 3 sequence.

## Day 3

*Step 1: Silent reading*

Return the underlined copy of the story to the student for a second silent reading. All known words should be underlined at this time. These second underlinings should be placed below the first and should be made using a different color marker. This step provides immediate evidence of growth that has taken place.

*Step 2: Oral reading*

Once the silent reading and underlining are completed, have the student read the story aloud again. Keep a record on the same copy used the previous day, using differently colored ink. This second record of oral reading provides more information about learning that has taken place and helps confirm judgements about areas needing further instruction.

*Step 3: Scrambled List I*

Continue the cycle of word learning by altering the context further with Scrambled List I. Prepare this list by taking *known* words from the Sequential List and mixing up their order. (Known words are those words recognized easily and without help during the reading of the Sequential List.) A Scrambled List I, made from "Frog," is illustrated in Figure 3-D.

*Figure 3-D*                          **Scrambled List I**

                                           **Frog**

                                  frog        day
                                  is          night
                                  he          asleep
                                  the

Since the words are not in the same order in which they appeared in the story, reading Scrambled List I is a more difficult task than reading the Sequential List, and it is important at this point to give the student every chance for success. Thus, in preparing Scrambled List I, do not use a strictly random order. Rather, begin and end the list with several words that will probably be easy for the student to recognize. Spread the more difficult words as evenly as possible throughout the rest of the list. It is usually not necessary to include duplicate words (words from the

Sequential List that appear more than once), but including such duplicates for some students can increase the chance for success. Have the student read Scrambled List I aloud, and again keep a record on a second copy of the list.

### Day 4

On the fourth day the student no longer needs to reread the original story. The only step is to present the *known*\*\* words from Scrambled List I in a new list, Scrambled List II, as illustrated for "Frog" in Figure 3-E.

*Figure 3-E*                    ***Scrambled List II***

Frog

| day | night |
|-----|-------|
| frog | he |
| asleep | |

Have the student read the list aloud, and keep a record of performance on another copy. Since so much of the original context has now been removed, this task is probably the most challenging, and the student may not know several words at this point that were recognized earlier. In order to keep the emphasis on success, after the list is completed, have the student reidentify one or two of the forgotten words by finding them in the original story and, if necessary, reading the sentences in which they appear. The sentence/story context will usually be all the student needs to recognize forgotten words.

### Day 5

The final step in this cycle is placing the known words from Scrambled List II on word cards for identification by the student. (Forgotten words that may have been reidentified by going back to the story are not included.) Prepare small, word-sized cards (see Figure 3-F) for all the words known on Scrambled List II.

*Figure 3-F*                    ***Word Bank Cards***

\*\*A scrambled list always contains only the known words from the previous list. If words were unknown in an earlier, easier task, it is unreasonable to expect recognition in a more difficult setting. If the unknown words are truly a part of the student's oral vocabulary, they are bound to appear in future dictation and can be learned then.

Cut up index cards work well for making word cards. Ask the student to read each of the cards. Each one that is identified immediately goes into the student's Word Bank, a small box sturdy enough to withstand much use. After a number of words have been accumulated, word cards may be filed in envelopes on which have been printed the letters of the alphabet. Keeping the words in order this way allows for good organization of the Word Bank and can reinforce learning of alphabetical order.

Once students have begun acquiring a sight vocabulary from dictated stories, they should be encouraged to transfer their learning to other-author materials. Make available a classroom library of books and magazines that match student interests, and have students spend some time daily browsing and reading these materials. Some students will find known words; others may only enjoy illustrations at first. As they make progress, students will be able to read these materials, and this practice will reinforce the work they are doing with their dictated stories.

To summarize, the basic cycle includes these student activities:

Day 1:    Dictate story
Day 2:    Read story silently
          Read story orally
          Read Sequential List
Day 3:    Read story silently
          Read story orally
          Read Scrambled List I
Day 4:    Read Scrambled List II
Day 5:    Read word cards
          Put cards in Word Bank
          Browse and read classroom library materials

### *Word Bank Activities*

As the basic dictation cycle is followed, students are given repeated contact with story words to aid retention of sight vocabularies. Rereading stories and working with structured lists assure some reinforcement; the Word Bank provides additional practice. Word Bank words are further removed from the context of the story than the story-derived lists. As such they can be used to develop immediate recognition of words independent of familiar associations. One or more of the following activities worked into each day's program will provide the necessary reinforcement. Some of these activities also encourage oral exchanges between students, reinforcing oral language skills.

1. Have students work in pairs to read aloud Word Bank words to one another.

2. Have students arrange their word cards in various categories; for example, things to eat, things that are alive, names of people.

3. Have students pair up and each choose two or three words from their Word Banks to show their partner. Students should talk about word meanings and personal associations with the words.

4. As students acquire new words for their Word Banks, have them work in groups to show the others these new words and talk about their meanings.

5. Give each student in a group an illustration from a magazine. Have the students go through their Word Banks to find words to go with the pictures; for example, color words or other descriptive words as well as various nouns and verbs. After each has found some words, have group members take turns showing their pictures and the accompanying words they have found.

### *Story Practice Activities*

While Word Bank work reinforces word learning, other activities are needed to emphasize the process of obtaining meaning from print. Simply reading dictated stories during the basic lesson cycle may not help students prepare for reading other-author materials. Other practice activities, related to dictations, can help students deal with their stories as they will later deal with other print materials. Activities such as these will ensure such practice.

1. Have two or more students select an appropriate story and present it to the class using creative dramatics or reader's theater techniques.

2. Have students select several related stories and copy them on a poster to produce a newspaper.

3. Copy student stories onto index cards. Place titles on separate cards. Shuffle each deck and have students match titles with the appropriate stories, discussing their reasons for making their choices.

4. Have students select stories to be corrected for "publication" and taken home to be shared with family and friends.

5. Have students read stories into a tape recorder to be used as read-along tapes by other students.

6. After a number of stories have been dictated about different topics, have the students organize them into chapters of a book, or produce individual books on topics such as "My Family" to be shared in the class library.

7. Copy a story onto individual sentence strips. Have students organize the strips in a logical order and then compare this sequence with the original story.

8. Have two or more students read and compare their stories about the same topic. Have them make a chart or drawing showing how their stories are the same and how they differ.

### *Other Language Activities*

Besides reinforcing reading skills with Word Banks and story-related activities Stage 2 students also need to continue developing oral language skills. The following activities are suitable for this additional practice; one or two of these should be included in each student's program several times a week.

1. Arrange a classroom library of easy-to-read books on a variety of topics. Encourage students to browse through the library, find known words in the materials, enjoy the illustrations, and talk to each other about the books.

2. Give students old newspapers and magazines and have them cut out known words to be arranged on a word poster. Encourage them to show their posters to other students and discuss their words.

3. Have several books and stories taped. Give students the opportunity to listen to these tapes as they follow along with the written text.

4. Have filmstrips or films available for viewing by one or more students. Encourage students to discuss and comment on what they see and hear. Filmstrips without accompanying sound will especially encourage students to talk to one another about their viewing.

5. Collect copies of students' dictated stories in a special folder. Encourage students to read their stories to one another or browse through the folder reading one another's stories.

6. Read aloud stories to small groups of students. Have them discuss/comment on what they liked about the stories and perhaps act out a scene or two, improvising actions and dialogue.

Several commercial programs designed for ESL students are available for developing oral English ability through a variety of listening, speaking, and reading activities. These may be used to supplement the Stage 2 student's work with dictated stories to expand speaking and reading vocabularies. Most are intended for young pupils (grades K-3), but the methods and activities may be adapted for students of all ages.

Garcia, Mary H. and Gonzales-Mena, Janet. *The Big E.* Silver Spring, MD: Institute for Modern Languages, 1976.

*Look, Listen, and Read Series: Sets 1, 2, and 3.* New York: ACI Productions, Inc., 1975.

McCallum, George P. *101 Word Games: For Students of English as a Second or Foreign Language.* New York: Oxford University Press, 1980.

Marquardt, William F.; Miller, Jean H.; and Hosman, Eleanore. *English Around the World.* Glenview, IL: Scott, Foresman, 1970.

*Read On Series: Sets 1 and 2.* New York: ACI Productions, Inc., 1975.

## SCHEDULING

By the time one story has been used for five lessons, work should already be underway on at least one additional story. With each new dictation, many previously used words will be used again, so each story tends to reinforce previous learning. Also, the valuable oral practice during discussion and dictation is as important in building reading skills as in learning more words from any one story. As oral English ability increases, the student finds it easier to read written English. It may be desirable with some rapid learners to start a new dictated story sequence every day. With other students it will be more advisable to begin a new story every second or third day. One possible schedule, including dictation and reinforcement activities, is illustrated in Table 3-1.

*Table 3-1*    ***Weekly Schedule for Dictation and Reinforcement Activities***

| day 1 | day 2 | day 3 |
|---|---|---|
| Story 1: dictate story | Story 1: read story silently; read story orally; sequential list | Story 1: read story silently; read story orally; scrambled list I |
| Browse through classroom library | | |
| Listen to tape of read-along book | Listen to other students read their stories | Story 2: dictate story |
| | | Tape record Story 1 |
| View/discuss filmstrip | Look through newspapers for known words; make word poster | Browse through classroom library |
| Word Bank activities | | |
| | Word Bank activities | Reorganize Story 1 from sentence strips |

| day 4 | day 5 |
|---|---|
| Story 1: scrambled list II | Story 1: Word Bank cards |
| Story 2: read story silently; read story orally; sequential list | Story 2: read story silently; read story orally; scrambled list I |
| Read aloud stories to other students | View/discuss filmstrip |
| Dramatize a story for the class | Listen to teacher-read story |
| Word Bank activities | Look through magazine for known words |
| | Word Bank activities |

This basic reading/language plan is designed to fit into a regular school day or tutoring session. It is important, however, to space the basic activivies as indicated, over several days' time, to avoid overloading the student with too much new learning material on any given day. The suggested schedule balances new learning and review each day; the plan can be altered to suit particular needs and schedules, but this same balancing principle should be the basis of whatever schedule is used.

# GROUP VS. INDIVIDUAL DICTATION

The plan just described outlines the steps for obtaining and working with one student's dictated stories. The same procedures may also be used with a small group of learners. Group discussion of an experience often stimulates greater oral language practice because each student contributes unique vocabulary and expressions to the discussion. Shy students can also be encouraged to use their still imperfect English when they see their peers' ideas accepted by the teacher. Students may also enjoy a group discussion more because they have several people to communicate with.

During group dictation each student should be encouraged to contribute to the story, but it is not always necessary to get a contribution from each. As long as each student is present during the discussion, the resulting dictation will be meaningful reading material for all.

Once the story is obtained, each student needs a chance to read the story silently and aloud. Several group readings should also be scheduled during the week for added reinforcement. Each student should underline known words, work through the structured lists, and obtain Word Bank cards for known words. This same basic plan should be followed for each student in the group.

Usually a student will retain fewer words from a group story than from one dictated individually. Other students' unique vocabulary and expressions may not be as easy to learn and remember, especially if one student's native language is different from another's. However, if the group is compatible, the advantages of working together and communicating with one another may outweigh language difference difficulties. Also, overall dictating time is shortened when a group composes a story instead of several individuals composing stories separately, allowing more time during the week for individual practice with the stories and word learning activities. The decision to use individual stories, group stories, or a combination of the two must be made by the teacher on the basis of student needs and the particular instructional setting.

# APPROPRIATE STIMULUS TOPICS

Stage 2 students, just beginning to refine oral English skills, need to discuss and dictate topics that are directly related to their daily activities and personal concerns. They need chances to use and reuse the English vocabulary they are acquiring; the more personally relevant their dictated stories are, the more easily they will acquire English skills. At this stage students should be encouraged to suggest their own topics for dictation as often as possible. Teachers might also suggest ideas that are clearly related to the students' immediate interests.

Here are some ideas for stimulus topics. These can easily be modified to suit the ages and interests of particular groups of students.

1. Take students on a walk around the school or neighborhood. Observe trees, plants, buildings, people, cars.

2. Engage students in a cooking lesson to prepare a simple dish. Talk about ingredients, utensils, and the fun of eating the finished product.

3. Show students a simple craft such as paper weaving or puppet making. Discuss items used to make the product and talk about each student's completed item.

4. Plant seeds to establish a classroom herb or flower garden. Each student may have one small pot to plant and tend, or the group may work together on a large planter. Talk about the various steps in the process and what must be done to care for the plants.

5. Have students take turns wearing a favorite item of clothing to school. Discuss why the student likes the special item, where it came from, how it is made, and so on.

6. Have students bring in photographs of family, friends, or neighborhood. Discuss the various items pictured; have students compare and contrast their photographs.

7. Put a mystery object in a paper bag. Have students try to guess what the object is by feeling (not looking). Discuss all the things that could be in the bag, given the features noted by feeling.

8. Set up a special display of shells, dried flowers, tools, health-care objects or a model train. Have students discuss what they see, hear, and feel as they examine the display.

Talking about an object or recent experience can be easy for many students, as object features (size, color, use) or vivid recollections can be readily identified and described. To illustrate use of various personal topics, we include here in Figure 3-G an example of a Stage 2 story and its illustration, one with vivid meaning for the student.

Any topic of interest to a learner can work well as a stimulus for dictation. The key to choosing a good stimulus will always be an understanding of the learner's particular tastes and interests. Repeated work with students will make choices easier as time goes on. Soon, students will also be suggesting dictation topics as they become familiar with the process.

Because Stage 2 students are also involved in learning about their new culture, dictation may be tied to lessons about such topics as American holidays and customs, typical seasonal activities in the local area, important U.S. or local historical events, geographic features of the

U.S., or significant American laws. Reading and listening experiences with a variety of good books can be used to introduce such topics. A list of suitable books appears below.***

*Figure 3-G*

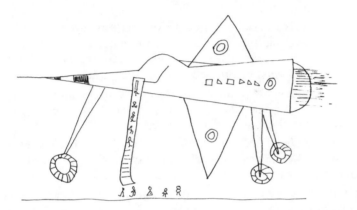

I came on a plane. My family, my daddy, my mother, my grandmother, my sister, my little . brother, my big brother and I. Seven of us came on a plane with 200 people from Cambodia.

## GENERAL INTEREST

Burnett, Bernice. *The First Book of Holidays* (revised edition). New York: Franklin Watts, Inc., 1974.

Rojankovsky, Feodor. *The Tall Book of Nursery Tales.* New York: Harper Row, 1944.

Turner, Philip. *Brian Wildsmith's Illustrated Bible Stories.* New York: Franklin Watts, Inc., 1968.

## LIFE IN THE UNITED STATES

Bradley, Duane. *The Newspaper: Its Place in a Democracy.* Princeton: D. Van Nostrand Co., Inc., 1965.

Kohn, Bernice. *The Spirit and the Letter: The Struggle for Rights in America.* New York: The Viking Press, 1974.

McGraith, Edward J. *A Child's History of America.* Boston: Little, Brown and Co., 1975.

***We thank Nancy Shibata, ESL teacher, Goleta, CA, for her assistance in compiling this list.

Miller, Stanley N. and Noble, Ruth. *The U.S.A. in Pictures.* New York: Sterling Publishing Company, Inc., 1975.

## HISTORICAL AMERICA

### Plymouth Colony

Bulla, Clyde. *John Billington, Friend of Squanto.* New York: T. Crowell, 1956.

_____. *Squanto.* New York: T. Crowell, 1954.

Clapp, Patricia. *Constance, A Story of Early Plymouth.* New York: Lothrop, Lee and Shepard Co., Inc., 1968.

Dalgliesh, Alice. *The Thanksgiving Story.* New York: Charles Scribner's Sons, 1954.

### The Frontier

Dalgliesh, Alice. *The Courage of Sarah Noble.* New York: Charles Scribner's Sons, 1954.

Fritz, Jean. *The Cabin Faced West.* New York: Coward, McCann and Geoghegan, Inc., 1958.

Laycock, George and Laycock, Ellen. *How the Settlers Lived.* New York: David McKay Co., Inc., 1980.

### The Revolution

Caudill, Rebecca. *Tree of Freedom.* New York: The Viking Press, 1949.

Dalgliesh, Alice. *Adam and the Golden Cock.* New York: Charles Scribner's Sons, 1959.

_____ . *The Fourth of July Story.* New York: Charles Scribner's Sons, 1956.

Forbes, Esther. *Johnny Tremain.* Boston: Houghton Mifflin, 1943.

Fritz, Jean. *What's the Big Idea, Ben Franklin?* New York: Coward, McCann and Geohegan, Inc., 1976.

Hays, Wilma Pitchford. *The Scarlet Badge.* New York: Holt, Rinehart and Winston Inc., 1963.

### The Civil War

Bacmeister, Rhoda. *Voices in the Night.* Indianapolis: Bobbs-Merrill Co., Inc., 1965.

Burchard, Peter. *Bimby.* New York: Coward-McCann, Inc., 1968.

DeAngeli, Marguerite. *Thee, Hannah!* Garden City, NY: Doubleday and Co., Inc., 1940.

Fox, Paula. *The Slave Dancer.* Scarsdale, NY: Bradbury Press, 1973.

Fritz, Jean. *Brady.* New York: Coward, McCann and Geoghegan, Inc., 1960.

Monjo, Ferdinand. *The Drinking Gourd.* New York: Harper and Row, 1970.

_____. *The Vicksburg Veteran.* New York: Simon and Schuster, Inc., 1971.

*Moving West*

Ball, Zachary. *North to Abilene.* New York: Holiday House, Inc., 1960.

Brenner, Barbara. *Wagon Wheels.* New York: Harper and Row, 1978.

Johnson, Annabel and Johnson, Edgar. *Torrie.* New York: Harper and Row, 1960.

Wilder, Laura Ingalls. *The Little House* series. New York: Harper and Row, 1953-71.

## TRANSITION TO STAGE 3

Most Stage 2 students need to continue the basic Stage 2 program for several months or longer to build strong abilities with oral English and to develop effective basic reading skills. Stage 2 students need numerous experiences working with a variety of dictated stories and practicing oral language skills in many different settings before they will be ready for more challenging Stage 3 procedures.

Generally, when students are consistently able to recognize at least 75% of the words on their first readings of dictated stories, they will be ready for Stage 3 procedures. Of course, attitude and psychological readiness must also be considered before moving students on to more difficult tasks. Besides good reading performance, the Stage 2 student should also demonstrate confidence when using English orally and when reading dictated stories and other materials in English. When these criteria are met, Stage 3 procedures may be introduced.

## SUMMARY

Stage 2 student reading skills are developed through student dictated stories used in a carefully sequenced cycle of lessons. The student is given repeated contact with the story and various word learning activities which help reinforce learning in meaningful contexts. Repeated dictations and various follow-up activities develop reading skills and allow assessment of oral language needs. The same basic plan may be used for individual or group instruction. Dictation topics may include subjects of personal, daily concern to the student and may also help the student acquire information about American culture.

## *REFERENCES*

Nessel, D. D., and Jones, M. B. *The Language-Experience Approach to Reading: A Handbook for Teachers.* New York: Teachers College Press, 1981.

Stauffer, R. G., Abrams, J. C., and Pikulski, J. J. *Diagnosis, Correction, and Prevention of Reading Disabilities.* New York: Harper and Row, 1978.

# Chapter 4

# The Stage 3 Student

The Stage 3 student has some ability to communicate in English and is a proficient speaker/reader in the native language or has been successful with Stage 2 reading/language procedures. Stage 3 students are often adolescents or adults who have had considerable schooling in their native countries, but a number of children will also be at this stage. These learners already understand the reading process. They do not need to learn to read but rather to refine reading abilities. These students are generally more self confident, having already experienced success as learners and can handle a somewhat more demanding program which emphasizes not only reading skills but also the subtleties of the language (idioms, colloquialisms) and various concepts that are presented in content area study.

## PROCEDURES FOR STAGE 3 STUDENTS

### Basic Teaching Plan

The teaching plan for Stage 3 learners is also based on dictated stories, constructed by student and teacher following a meaningful experience. The teacher then helps the student rephrase ideas so that the story conforms to common English usage standards. Reading skills and oral language ability are developed together, using dictated stories as the basic reading materials and as models of proper English usage. The student reads his orally-produced story, insuring that the written message is meaningful.

#### Day 1

*Step 1: Taking dictation*

Follow the same procedures for discussing a topic or experience and taking dictation as those outlined for the Stage 2 learner. Make two copies of the story for instructional use. Once these steps have been completed, make notes of usage and vocabulary difficulties that occur in the dictated story to assess the student's language needs. The story and record sheet in Figure 4-A illustrate these first steps.

*Figure 4-A*                              ***Original story***

> My friends is in the beach. They are looking to the north. And they think that the people that live there is having cold. They are looking for shells. Too they swam one time. They eat very much because they have hungry. The ocean is blue and sometimes it looks green.

### *Assessment of needs*

1. use of prepositions *on* and *in*
2. use of phrases *to be hungry, to be cold* and others with the same construction
3. use of *also* and *too*
4. review of subject-verb agreement
5. uses of *that* and *who*
6. vocabulary ("They swam one time" although not incorrect can be said less awkwardly.)

## Day 2

### *Step 1: Rereading the story*

Show the student one copy of the story, keeping the record sheet nearby for reference and additions. Read the story aloud exactly as it is written; help the student follow by pointing to the words and phrases while reading smoothly at a normal pace to provide a model of fluent English. Then have the student read the story silently and then orally. Some students may not be able to master the story at this point and will need to do additional readings with teacher help. Make these readings as supportive and encouraging as possible. Do not correct errors.

### *Step 2: Revising the story**

Recopy the story on a fresh sheet of paper, stopping to call attention to the first usage or vocabulary error in the story. Explain the correct way of stating the idea and have the student repeat the corrected statement several times. For example, the teacher working with the story in Figure 4-A might say:

> We can say this first idea a little better. We say, "My friends are at the beach." "Are" is what we say when we mean more than one ... my friends *are*. And "at the beach" is better than "in the beach." Say it after me ... my friends are at the beach.

*We thank Matilde Sanchez-Villalpando, Oxnard Community College, Oxnard, CA, for sharing with us her strategies for revising dictated stories obtained from ESL students.

It is best to avoid a rules-based explanation for corrections. That is, the teacher in this exchange did not explain that friends is third person plural and therefore takes a third person plural verb, are. Rather, the explanation is kept simple and the emphasis is on having the student repeat (imitate) the correct usage.

Once the correction has been explained and repeated by the student, write the corrected statement while the student watches. Then ask the student to read the revised statement as completed. Continue this procedure until the entire story is recopied. It is not always necessary or advisable to correct every error. If there are many errors in a long story, choose a few of the most significant to work with. Regardless of how many corrections are made, it is important that the student feel involved in the revisions, not just a passive recipient of corrections. Occassionally it may be desirable to have the student suggest another way of saying an idea so that all corrections do not originate with the teacher. Figure 4-B shows the corrected version of the beach story.

*Figure 4-B*                     ***Revised story***

My friends are at the beach. They are looking to the north. And they think that the people who live there are having cold weather. They are looking for shells. Also they swam one time. They eat very much because they are hungry. The ocean is blue and sometimes it looks green.

***Oral reading assessment***

Unknown words:   weather
                 very
                 sometimes
Pronunciation difficulties:
1. the English /r/ in words like friends, north, hungry, green
2. the difference between /sh/ and /ch/ (uses them interchangeably)

## Step 3: Silent reading

After corrections have been made, have the student read the corrected story silently, underlining any unknown words.** As with Stage 2 students, Stage 3 students may also overestimate or underestimate what they know. With encouragement and acceptance, most students will soon learn to underline only those words they actually do not know and thus come to assess their own abilities realistically.

## Step 4: Oral reading

Finally, have the student read the story aloud, giving help on any unknown words. During this oral reading, keep notes on the record sheet

**For Stage 3 learners the focus is on unknown words rather than known words because, with their basic understanding of the reading process (from native language learning), they are not threatened by emphasis on unfamiliar words at this point.

of unknown words, pronunciation difficulties, and other needs still
evident.*** Keep the record sheet and the corrected copy of the story for
later comparisons. Figure 4-B illustrates the record sheet that
accompanies the corrected beach story.

## Day 3

*Step 1: Silent reading*
First give the student a copy of the corrected story to be read
silently. Any unknown words should be underlined. This underlining can
be compared with that of the previous day to assess progress. Some
students may have forgotten several words at this point and may need
support to overcome discouragement.

*Step 2: Oral reading*
Now have the student read the story aloud. Give prompt help with
any unknown words, anticipating difficulties by noting which words the
student has underlined. Supply help with words quickly to maintain
fluent reading. The student should read the story several times until s/he
is able to read it through with good fluency and little help. During these
readings continue to note any difficulties.

## Day 4

*Step 1: Silent reading*
Give the student the same copy of the story used on Day 3 to read
silently, again underlining any unknown words. This second underlining
might be done with a different colored pen to make it easier to note
growth from the previous day.

*Step 2: Oral reading*
Once again, have the student read the story aloud, giving prompt
help on any unknown or forgotten words. Several readings will allow
most students to read the story through easily alone.

*Step 3: Self correction*
Now give the student the second, unmarked copy of the *original*
story to be read silently. Have the student orally or in writing make
needed corrections in usage and vocabulary. Having spent several days
working with the revised story, the student will usually be able to make
these corrections easily. If there is any difficulty, have the student refer to
the familiar, corrected version of the story. Such self correction reinforces

---

***If at this point the student fails to identify correctly at least 75% of the
story words, these Stage 3 procedures are inappropriate for the student. Work
with Stage 2 activities is needed.

new learning and demonstrates clearly how much the student has gained since the original dictation.

Figures 4-C, 4-D, and 4-E illustrate three dictated stories obtained from adolescent Stage 3 students. The needs assessments and revisions of the dictations are also included for each.

*Figure 4-C*                      ***Original story***

    My friends went to the beach last summer. This beach is in California. They drink soda. They collected shells. They have camera and take the pictures. They swam in the ocean and saw many sharks. They had afraid. They stayed in the beach four weeks. They are tired. They slept for one day.

***Revised story***

    My friends went to the beach last summer. This beach is in California. They drank soda. They collected shells. They have a camera and take pictures. They swam in the ocean and saw many sharks. They were afraid. They stayed at the beach four weeks. They are tired. They slept for one day.

***Assessment of needs***

1. use of articles *a* and *the*
2. use of linking verbs and predicate adjectives (*were* afraid instead of *have* afraid)
3. use of prepositions (*on* the beach instead of *in* the beach)

*Figure 4-D*                      ***Original story***

    They went to the city. Then they went to the discotheque and they danced very much. They saw in the discotheque a John Travolta. Silvia danced with him. Then Mati dance with him. In the discotheque drank wine and then drank coca-cola. Then went to the restaurant and they ate in the restaurant soup, chicken, potatoes, and salad.

***Revised story***

    They went to the city. Then they went to the discotheque and they danced a lot. In the discotheque they saw John Travolta. Silvia danced with him. Then Mati danced with him. In the discotheque they drank wine and then drank coca-cola. Then they went to the restaurant and there they ate soup, chicken, potatoes, and salad.

***Assessment of needs***

1. use of subjects in sentences [(they) drank wine. . .(they) went to the restaurant]
2. verb tense (Mati *danced* with him)
3. awkward phrasing (*they danced very much* may be improved, as may be the positioning of prepositional phrases, e.g., *they saw in the discotheque* and *they ate in the restaurant*)

*Figure 4-E*                      ***Original story***

    This is my family. We are live in San Luis Potosi city. We are Mexican. Sometimes we are play baseball. Ever my father plays with me. We have two teams. Mine are my brother, my sister, and I. We are the champions. My

*Figure 4-E cont.*

mother never wants to play with we. She prefer stays in home for make to eat.

### Revised story
This is my family. We are living in the city of San Luis Potosi. We are
Mexican. Sometimes we play baseball. My father always plays with us. We
have two teams. My brother, my sister, and I are one team. We are the
champions. My mother never wants to play with us, she prefers to stay home
to make us things to eat.

### Assessment of needs
1. verb forms (*are live, are play,* and *she prefer* need revision)
2. use of objective pronouns (*us* instead of *we*)
3. awkward/incorrect constructions (*stays in home for make to eat; ever my
   father; we have two teams. . .mine are*)

The students were shown pictures of people walking on a beach, eating in
a restaurant, and wearing baseball equipment, repectively. Each was
encouraged to make up a story about the picture. The resulting dictations
illustrate the variety of English vocabulary and language patterns that
these students were able to use and also reveal several of the kinds of
usage errors that may occur at this stage. The dictations are
representative of Stage 3 stories, demonstrating relatively good mastery of
oral English and expressive fluency. The stories also reflect assimilation
of various concepts typical of American culture.

Examination of the revisions shows that there can be several ways to
revise incorrect or awkward phrases or sentences. It will be up to the
teacher to decide how to revise various constructions. Revisions should
retain the student's original meaning and as many of the original words
as possible. On occasion, new words must be added to phrase the idea
well; for example, in Figure 4-E the word *things* was added to the story
in revising the final sentence. When such new words are to be added,
words already familiar to the student or relatively common words should
be used whenever possible.

Needs assessments may also be done in several different ways. It is
most useful to categorize the errors instead of simply listing them.
Categorization will make it easier, after several stories have been
obtained, to review needs and plan instruction to improve oral language.
For instance, if several stories reveal difficulties with prepositions, verb
forms, or some other type of error, instruction can be planned to cover
that element of usage.

## Follow-up Activities

Stage 3 students need recontact with story words and with dictated
stories to reinforce and maintain learning. A number of follow-up

activities are useful for this. For instance:

1. Keep a separate folder in the classroom for extra copies of dictated stories. Encourage students to browse through these and read them to one another.
2. Have students make their own dictionaries in which they list newly learned words. Definitions may be dictated, or students may write their own; illustrations may be drawn or cut from old magazines. Encourage students to use several illustrations as different examples of the words to reinforce the concept. For example, *television aerial* can be illustrated with pictures of different types of aerials; *automobile* could be illustrated with pictures of different car models.
3. Prepare a matching game in which printed word cards can be matched with cut out illustrations. Have students work independently or in pairs to play.
4. Use teacher written stories, including words from student dictated stories, as additional reading materials.
5. Give students copies of dictated stories from which words have been omitted; have them fill in the omitted words as they read the stories.

A variety of follow-up activities may be planned for each dictation, allowing different kinds of recontact with the story and practice with story words in other contexts. To illustrate, Figures 4-F through 4-I show one story dictated by a group of five Stage 3 students and the teacher-designed activities to accompany it.

*Figure 4-F*                    **Noa, Tung, and Amburi**

A girl named Noa lives in Thailand. She is twenty years old. She has two brothers, Nuk Tung and Nuk Amburi. Tung is fifteen years old and Amburi is sixteen years old. Noa and her family are farmers. They grow bananas and coconuts. Coconuts grow on palm trees. They also keep chickens.

One day Noa goes into the garden. Noa sees the bananas and the coconuts. She sees a monkey eating a banana in a tree. Noa calls her brother, Amburi, and tells him to bring his bow and arrows. Amburi aims his bow and arrow at the monkey and fires. He hits the monkey in the heart. The monkey falls down dead. Amburi brings the monkey home to his mother. His mother cooks the monkey and everyone eats the monkey. They also eat rice, fruit, celery, tea, and soy sauce. Everyone says that is a good monkey.

After dinner everyone goes to sleep. Nuk Tung has a dream about his girlfriend in Thailand. Her name is Ah. He dreams that they are walking in the garden together. He dreams that he sees a monkey in a tree eating a banana and that he kills it with his bow and arrow. Ah says, "I am very happy because you killed the monkey that was in the garden."

The sun comes up and Nuk Tung wakes up. Tung goes to the garden. He thinks to himself, "Maybe I will dance. . ." But he doesn't dance.

*Figure 4-G*                          ***Cloze exercise:***

**Noa, Tung, and Amburi**

A girl named Noa _____ in Thailand. She is _____ years old. She has _____ brothers, Nuk Tung and _____ Amburi. Tung is fifteen _____ old and Amburi is _____ years old. Noa and _____ family are farmers. They _____ bananas and coconuts. Coconuts _____ on palm trees. They _____ keep chickens.

One day _____ goes into the garden. _____ sees the bananas and _____ coconuts. She sees a _____ eating a banana in _____ tree. Noa calls her _____ Amburi and tells him _____ bring his bow and _____ . Amburi aims his bow _____ arrow at the monkey _____ fires. He hits the _____ in the heart. The _____ falls down dead. Amburi _____ the monkey home to _____ mother. His mother cooks _____ monkey and everyone eats _____ monkey. They also eat _____ , fruit, celery, tea, and _____ sauce. Everyone says that _____ a good monkey.

*(Note: This is a true cloze as every 5th word is left out.)*

*Figure 4-H*                          ***Word identification:***

**Noa, Tung, and Amburi**

| | | | |
|---|---|---|---|
| fruit | _____ | tea | _____ |
| coconuts | _____ | soy sauce | _____ |
| monkey | _____ | bananas | _____ |
| celery | _____ | chickens | _____ |
| palm trees | _____ | rice | _____ |

*Figure 4-1*          ***Classification exercise:***

**Noa, Tung, and Amburi**

| Food | Animals | People |
|------|---------|--------|
| ____ | ____ | ____ |
| ____ | ____ | ____ |
| ____ | ____ | ____ |
| ____ | ____ | ____ |
| ____ | ____ | ____ |
| ____ | ____ | ____ |

|       |         |          |
|-------|---------|----------|
| girl    | Amburi   | chickens |
| rice    | celery   | mother   |
| fruit   | bananas  | Ah       |
| brothers| Noa      | Tung     |
| monkey  | coconuts |          |

As students' oral English skills improve, additional strategies may be used to stimulate learning of new vocabulary. A particularly useful technique at this point is a modification of Calvert's (1974) "key vocabulary" approach, which helps students extend their learning beyond dictated stories based on personal experience. The basic steps are:

1. Conduct a lesson to introduce a new concept (a science lesson on cloud formation, a mathematics lesson on proportions, or a discussion of character development in a story or film). Following the lesson, have students brainstorm a list of words used in the discussion. List these on the chalkboard or on a large sheet of chart paper. Help the students, when necessary, by reminding them of the different concepts that were addressed. Students may not recall all of the most important words from the lesson and should not be expected to do so. Accept any words the students do think of; those words that are most prominent in the student's minds will be the ones easiest for them to learn.

2. Have the group categorize the words, grouping them in whatever categories are logical for the topic. (One category may also be "miscellaneous" to cover words that do not fit into any established categories.) Record the categorized words near the original list.

3. Have students work in small groups to discuss and use the words in several ways. One or more categories may be assigned to each group. Some activities at this point may be:

    a. Have students make a word card for each of the words and then take turns displaying one card at a time to the rest of the group. The presenter should pronounce the word and either use it in a sentence or tell about the word's meaning.

    b. Have each group compose a picture dictionary page for each word in the group's collection. In order to do this, the group must discuss each word, agree on a simple definition, and decide how to illustrate the word. They may wish to draw pictures or may also search for illustrations in old newspapers or magazines. Students may write their definitions or may dictate them. Dictionary pages from all the groups can then be collected and fastened together; students should be encouraged to browse through the dictionary to reinforce learning.

   c. Ask students to compose a story or account using as many words in their collection as possible. The account may be written by the group or dictated. Groups can share their stories with one another, taking turns reading silently and aloud.

   d. Have students make up a matching exercise using the words in their collections. The groups must think of definitions for each of their words; these can be listed (written by the students or dictated) in one column while the words can be listed in mixed-up order in another column. Groups can share their exercises with one another.

4. Once students have discussed the key words and done one or more of the reinforcement activities, the groups may be gathered together again for a final dictation activity. Students should be asked to dictate a short account covering the main aspects of the original lesson. They will use many of the words they have been studying since they will have become familiar with their pronunciation and meaning. The account may be duplicated and given to each student for further study. Several of these dictations following an activity or a unit of study will help students review their learning in the subject while reinforcing and extending their learning of key words. Instead of group stories, individual dictations from each student may also be taken.

## *APPROPRIATE STIMULUS TOPICS*

While Stage 1 and Stage 2 students need to acquire vocabulary and concepts directly related to daily needs and highly personal interests, Stage 3 students, because of their relatively advanced oral English skills, can handle a broader range of topics and experiences for dictation and for vocabulary study. First-hand experiences and favorite interests, of course, can serve as the base of the Stage 3 program. But these students can also profit from discussing and dictating a variety of topics related to English materials they hear or read. Accounts and stories by other authors can serve as good models of English for these students while broadening their knowledge and experience.

We have found the sources listed below for dictation topics to be very good for generating interest and stimulating dictated stories and vocabulary study for Stage 3 students.

*Content Area Materials*

While Stage 3 students are increasing understanding and use of English during reading/language arts classes, they are also usually engaged in other areas of study, such as social studies, mathematics, and science. Materials from these lessons may serve as excellent stimuli for discussion and dictation during the reading/language arts period, as illustrated by the key vocabulary lesson previously outlined. The extra review of other studies is also valuable for reinforcing learning in these other areas. Many possibilities for working with the different subject areas can be explored. For example:

1. Have students dictate descriptions of science experiments. On their own copies of these dictations, have students illustrate the different steps in the process.
2. Have students dictate key events in history. These may be simple explanations of the main things that happened or may take on livelier forms, such as a dictated make-believe dialogue between key personalities in historic situations.
3. Have students dictate their own story problems to supplement their mathematics lessons. Small groups may dictate different problems and then exchange their arithmetic stories with other groups.

*Literature*

Good stories, written in English, can be used as the basis for many interesting dictation sessions. Fables or fairy tales from English-speaking cultures will usually fascinate students seeking to learn more about their new society. Similar tales, translated into English from their own or other cultures, will also be of interest to these learners. Library books and magazines will also provide many enjoyable contemporary stories. Simple, short tales may be read by the students; longer or more difficult stories may be read aloud by the teacher. In either case, discussion of the story and of the students' reaction to it will suggest many dictation topics. Students may want to retell the story in their own words, compose a new ending to a favorite story, or describe their reactions to the characters and events of the story.

Storytelling activities can also introduce the Stage 3 student to common English language tales and fables as will as reinforce English vocabulary and language patterns. Horne (1980) offers a workbook to help the teacher develop storytelling skills; many stories are included with suggestions for accompanying activities. Student dramatization of stories

and student-told stories, both excellent for developing oral language
skills, are emphasized in this resource material. We also recommend the
following materials as good sources for stories to tell to ESL students.
These tales from several cultures may be familiar to some of the students.
The multicultural emphasis may also serve as a good complement to
stories based on English-speaking cultures.

*Collections from a country or region:*

Bang, Garrett. *Men from the Village Deep in the Mountains and
Other Japanese Folk Tales.* New York: Macmillan, 1973.

Barlow, Genevieve. *Latin American Tales from the Pampas to the
Pyramids of Mexico.* New York: Rand McNally, 1966.

Buck, Pearl S., ed. *Fairy Tales of the Orient.* New York: Simon and
Schuster, 1965.

Caiswell, Hume Lotta. *Favorite Children's Stories from China and
Tibet.* Vermont: Charles E. Tuttle, Co., 1962.

Haviland, Virginia. *Favorite Fairy Tales Told in -----.* Boston:
Little, Brown (India, 1973; Sweden, 1966; Greece, 1970;
Czechoslovakia, 1966; Denmark, 1971; Scotland, 1963).

Nahdevi, Ann Sinclair. *Persian Folk and Fairy Tales.* New York:
Alfred A. Knopf, 1965.

Pratt, Davis, and Kula, Elsa. *Magic Animals of Japan.* Emeryville,
CA: Parnassus Press, 1967.

Reed, Gwendolyn. *The Talkative Beasts, Myths, Fables and Poems
of India.* New York: Lothrop, Lee and Shepard, 1969.

Sakade, Florence, ed. *Japanese Children's Favorite Stories.*
Vermont: Charles E. Tuttle Co., 1958.

*Collections from around the world:*

Baker, Augusta. *Talking Trees and Other Tales.* New York:
Lippincott, 1955.

Belting, Natalia. *The Sun is a Golden Earring.* New York: Holt,
Rinehart & Winston, 1962.

_____. *Calendar Moon.* New York: Holt, Rinehart &
Winston, 1964.

_____. *The Earth is on a Fish's Back.* New York: Holt,
Rinehart & Winston, 1965.

Dorson, Richard M. *Folk Tales Told Around the World.* Chicago:
University of Chicago Press, 1915.

Thompson, Stith. *One Hundred Favorite Folktales.* Bloomington,
IN: Indiana University Press, 1974.

## Films and Filmstrips

Films and filmstrips on a variety of topics can serve as an excellent source of ideas for dictation. Accounts of American wild animals, film tours of different parts of the U.S., amusing cartoons, or dramatized stories offer only a few of the many possibilities. Films supplement students' growing understanding of English with vivid pictures to aid comprehension of the story or account. St. Martin (1978) suggests providing students with printed copies of the film's narration the day before the film is shown. Reading such scripts with teacher assistance can help students prepare for viewing; discussion and rereading of the script after viewing can precede dictation. Morley and Lawrence (1971, 1972) present additional ideas for using films with ESL students.

*Oral History*

Students will usually be eager to talk about the culture and history of their hometowns. They will also be interested in comparing and contrasting this information with the history of the place in the U.S. to which they have moved. These interests can be tapped as another good source of dictation topics if oral history units are planned. Oral history projects involve interviewing residents of an area to learn what they know and what they remember about the people, customs, and historical happenings of the place. Adapted for the Stage 3 student, oral history projects could take these various forms:

1. Students could interview one another to learn about the various cultures from which each came.
2. Students could work with American-born students to interview long time residents of the local area to learn about the history of their new home.
3. Students could interview various teachers in the school (especially those who have lived and taught in the area for some time) to learn about the history of the school.
4. Students could interview their parents or other family members about their homeland.

Interviews may be taped, if desired, and the students can play the tapes and discuss their findings in class in preparation for dictation. If several students complete such projects, the resulting dictations may be bound in books for sharing with classmates and others.

This kind of project can encourage the students to practice their English in realistic communication settings, and much interesting information can be collected. The students might even be encouraged to photograph the people they talk to so that personal illustrations may accompany their dictations.

Several sources of information about oral history units are available to aid planning, for instance, Hartley and Shumway (1973), Hirsch and Lewinger (1975), and Neuenschwander (1976). These procedures, designed for American-born students, may be modified for ESL students.

To illustrate the use of a variety of stimulus topics for dictation with Stage 3 learners, we give some examples of dictation situations that encouraged students to use and learn words from a variety of sources.

In the first example, a group of Stage 3 learners had studied the history of the atomic explosion on Hiroshima. The main source of information was John Hersey's book, *Hiroshima,* which the group read with the teacher. (Some parts were read by the students, and some were read aloud by the teacher, depending on the difficulty of the various sections.) Following the reading and a good bit of discussion, the group dictated the story in Figure 4-J.

*Figure 4-J*

### Hiroshima

A flash! There was a bunch of dust. The wind after the flash. People's skin starts to burn. Buildings fall. People are killed. There is a big fire in the middle of town when the bomb hit. Nobody knows it's an atomic bomb. People think they are being bombed but it is only one bomb. Dr. Fuji lay in dreadful pain. Father La Salle he helped a lot of people get out of the ruins. Dr. Fuji helped a lot by putting bandages on their injuries.

There is a storm and flood and a lot of people drowned. Father La Salle made a raft to go across the river to try and save people that were drowning. He reached for a lady's hand and her skin just comes off and he sat there staring at her for a couple of minutes. She drowned.

After the storm there is a lot of dead bodies floating around. A strange disease starts to wipe out the people. People go back to their houses to see if they can get their belongings.

The center where the bomb hit the clay tiles melted. The melting point is one thousand three hundred degrees (1,300) centigrade. Radiation reading was 1.5 at the highest. It was really hot about 104 degrees. It was night and this little girl told the father she is cold. He took off his jacket and gave it to the little girl and she said she was still cold. She died after that.

No one knew about the radiation. Radiation killed a lot of people. We learned if there is a nuclear war there will be a disaster. 78,150 people were killed at Hiroshima, 13,983 people were missing and 37,425 people were injured.

The story not only illustrates their growing mastery of oral English but also reveals how vivid this story was to these students.

In the second example, a group of ten older Stage 3 students spent time learning words and behaviors associated with typical American social events. One day they discussed attending a dinner party in an American home, which each student had done or was planning to do. After discussing several key words (host, hostess, delicious food, knife, fork, napkin, etc.), the teacher presented a dinner party problem: being served a personally distasteful food. The problem came from a collection of similar situations (Kettering, 1975) designed for ESL learners. The students read the problem with teacher help and then worked in small groups to decide on the best solution to this awkward situation. Several possible solutions were suggested following the statement of the problem in the book; students were also encouraged to think of their own solutions. Each group then role-played the scene to illustrate their solution and explained why they would solve the problem in that particular way. Further discussion included general talk about American eating customs and tastes, proper guest behavior, and so on. Finally students dictated individual accounts about the classroom activity. These dictations reveal their varying reactions to the activity and the topic of the lesson and also illustrate the immediate use of words and phrases introduced and used during the lesson.

> The book talks about what we should say when we are served our dislike food or when we can't eat much more. It seems that American people appear their feelings straight. And if we do so, they will not feel bad.

> This book talks about how we can express our dislikeness of food. It shows five solutions, for example. We discuss about this situation and find out what to do.

> This book shows the examples of action when the host and hostess serve food we don't like to eat. Through comparing these examples we can find out which one is best.

> In this class we talked about being polite and behaving best when we are invited to dinner with American family and are served disliking food.

> An American family invited a guest to their dinner. Though hostess has made a special dinner for him and has used her best dishes and tablecloth, liver was served, which was hard for him to eat. The guest was explaining to her that he didn't like liver.

> The person who was invited to dinner doesn't like liver. But hostess don't know that and serve him liver. She wants him to eat very happily.

> I think it is bad manner to keep silent while we're eating. We should give the hostess some compliments about food which is served. They served too much, so I can't eat all of the food but I try to. Cake is too sweet.

> You had better say yes or no clearly when the host family ask you whether you like it or not. When you have dinner with an American family, you shouldn't be silent and should talk about a lot of things.

> When I had dinner with my host family, I said to them,
> "I like this very much" even in the case I don't like it
> very much. Taste in America is too sweet. For example,
> ice cream and chocolate cake. And American one dish is
> much more than Japanese one.

We have given the original dictations, uncorrected, to illustrate the level
of English usage and vocabulary of these Stage 3 students. The usual
procedures for revising the dictations to conform to regular usage would
be followed as the lessons proceeded.

## OTHER LANGUAGE ACTIVITIES

Other language activities may provide additional practice reading the
stories while developing reading-study skills such as selecting a main idea,
recognizing significant details, and sequencing events. Activities like these
will provide that practice and should be included in the basic program
several times a week:

1. Copy student stories onto large index cards without
   accompanying titles. Have students discuss the stories and think
   of several titles for each story. Guide students to think of different
   titles to suit different purposes; for example, a catchy title to
   stimulate interest in reading the story, a title that conveys the
   main idea, or a title that emphasizes a particular story feature.
   (Provide several titles for students if they have trouble thinking of
   them on their own.)
2. Select a story with a clear sequence of events. Have students
   make a time line for that story, listing the events in chronological
   order on a time line chart.
3. Have students go through old dictated stories and underline facts
   in one color and opinions in another color.
4. Have two or more students read and compare their stories on the
   same topic. Then have them cut apart their respective stories and
   compose a new story, combining statements from each of the
   original stories. They will have to reorder details, delete some
   repetitious statements, and consider the best way to organize the
   new story.
5. Have students take turns reading their stories to one another or a
   group and then asking the listener(s) two or three questions about
   the story content.

Cartoons and comic strips from local newspapers can also be
excellent sources of other language activities. Comic strips and cartoons
often introduce idioms, colloquialisms, and other language structures not
found in formal textbooks. These materials also show various aspects of

American life and humor that can be instructive and entertaining for ESL students. Elkins and Bruggeman (1971), Fowles (1970), and Swain (1978) present several ideas for using cartoons and comic strips. Schmelter (1972) presents a variation—using old coloring books as sources of discussion and language activities for the ESL student—which may also be appropriate for some Stage 3 students.

A number of commercial programs, designed for ESL students, are available for developing and refining oral English ability through a variety of listening, speaking, and reading activities. These may be used to supplement the Stage 3 student's work with dictated stories to expand speaking and reading vocabularies. Most are intended for older students (upper elementary through high school), but the methods and activities may be adapted for students of all ages.

Christison, Mary Ann and Bassano, Sharron. *Look Who's Talking!* San Francisco: The Alemany Press, 1981.

Dixson, Robert J. *Essential Idioms in English.* New York: Regents, 1971.

Finocchiaro, Mary. *Learning to Use English: Books I and II.* New York: Regents, 1966-68.

Fried Lee, Lauri E. *This is English.* San Francisco: The Alemany Press, 1982.

Hall, Eugene and Costinet, Sandra. *Orientation in American English: Levels I-VI.* Silver Spring, MD: Institute for Modern Languages, 1977.

Romijn, Elizabeth and Seely, Contee. *Live Action English for Foreign Students.* San Francisco: The Alemany Press, 1979.

Schurer, Linda, ed. *Everyday English.* San Francisco: The Alemany Press, 1977.

Slager, William R. *English for Today: Books I-VI.* New York: McGraw-Hill, 1972.

## *SUMMARY*

Stage 3 student reading skills are developed through dictated stories that are revised, with teacher help, to conform to standard English usage. Vocabulary is expanded through oral language activities and through modified "key vocabulary" study. Topics for discussion and dictation range from personal experiences through content area study, literature, and other sources of extended language usage. The same basic plan may be used for individual or group instruction.

# REFERENCES

Calvert, J. D. "Language experience as an affective and cognitive mobilizer to learning in the secondary classroom." Paper presented at the 8th Conference of the California Reading Association, San Diego, 1974.

Elkins, R. J., and Bruggemann, C. *Comic strips in the teaching of English as a foreign language.* Paper presented to a conference on the teaching of English, Kassel, West Germany ERIC REPORTS: ED 056 591, February, 1971.

Fowles, J. "Ho, Ho, Ho: Cartoons in the Language Class." *TESOL Quarterly,* June, 1970, *4*, 155-60.

Hartley, W. G., & Shumway, G. L. *An Oral History Primer.* Salt Lake City: The Author's Box, 1973.

Hirsch, R., and Lewinger, M. "Oral History: The family is the curriculum." *Teacher,* November, 1975, *93*, 60-62.

Horne, C. *Word Weaving: A Storytelling Workbook.* San Francisco: The Zellerbach Family Fund, 1980.

Kettering, J. C. *Developing Communication Competence: Interaction Activities in English as a Second Language.* Pittsburgh: University of Pittsburgh Center for International Studies, 1975.

Morley, H.J., and Lawrence, M.S. "The use of films in teaching English as a second language." *Language and Learning,* June, 1971, *22,* 117-135.

Morley, H.J., and Lawrence, M.S. "The use of films in teaching English as a second language." *Language and Learning,* June, 1972, *22,* 99-110.

Neuenschwander, J. *Oral History as a Teaching Approach.* Washington, D.C.: National Education Association, 1976.

St. Martin, G. M. *Films in the ESL classroom.* Paper presented at the annual conference of the National Association for Foreign Student Affairs, Iowa State University, ERIC REPORTS: ED 159 916, June, 1978.

Schmelter, H. "Teaching English to Mexican American students." *Today's Education,* March, 1972, *61*, 41.

Swain, E. H. "Using comic books to teach reading and language arts." *Journal of Reading,* December, 1978, *22,* 255-58.

# Chapter 5

# Word Recognition

Word recognition is an essential component in comprehending written language. To understand a writer's message, the reader must be able to move quickly through the text, recognizing most words immediately and figuring out unfamiliar words efficiently. To do this, the reader must acquire a store of instantly recognized words and must learn effective use of a variety of word recognition skills for independently identifying unknown words.

Some words are learned by *sight*; that is, the learner memorizes the word as a whole, connecting that particular configuration of letters with the given orally known word. English words with irregular spellings, like "colonel," are usually learned in this way since they cannot easily be broken into recognizable parts for analysis. Learning these words by sight is the most efficient learning method. Other words are learned by sight because they are encountered so often or are so meaningful to the student that whole word recognition takes place almost automatically. Learning to recognize one's name in print, for example, usually is the result of such meaningful, almost automatic learning.

In Chapters 2 through 4 we outlined the way ESL students establish reading vocabularies with dictated stories and various reinforcement activities. All the procedures emphasize sight learning in meaningful contexts. The teacher reads dictated stories with students and uses Sequential and Scrambled Lists and Word Banks to reinforce sight learning by giving students repeated exposure to the familiar words. Students are not asked to puzzle over unfamiliar words. This helps the ESL student acquire a store of easily recognized English words rather quickly and easily and also builds student confidence in handling written English. As students become more comfortable reading English, however, they need to learn additional word recognition skills so they can figure out words independently, that is, without relying on the teacher.

There are several ways in which readers independently identify unfamiliar words. They may use phonetic analysis (*phonics*) to "sound out" words, attaching sounds to letters or groups of letters to figure out the pronunciation of words and thus work towards identifying word meaning. Readers may also use *structural analysis,* breaking words into recognizable syllables or roots and affixes, which offer clues to meaning. Or readers may employ *context clues,* using other words and language patterns to identify a particular word. Picture clues and other graphic aids are also forms of context clues which help readers identify unfamiliar words.

Teaching independent word recognition strategies is in itself the topic of much research and many books. We will not attempt to deal in depth with the entire subject but will only suggest some general strategies and note issues of particular concern. For those interested in further reading, here are some sources:

*Teacher materials:*

> Coley, Joan D. and Gambrell, Linda B. *Programmed Reading Vocabulary for Teachers.* Columbus: Charles Merrill, 1977.
>
> Durkin, Dolores. *Strategies for Identifying Words.* Boston: Allyn and Bacon, 1976.
>
> Heilman, Arthur. *Phonics in Proper Perspective.* Columbus: Charles Merrill, 1981.
>
> Ives, Josephine, Bursuk, Laura, and Ives, Sumner. *Word Identification Techniques.* Chicago: Rand McNally, 1979.
>
> Johnson, Dale and Pearson, P. David. *Teaching Reading Vocabulary.* New York: Holt, Rinehart and Winston, 1978.
>
> Wilson, Robert M. and Hall, MaryAnne. *Programmed Word Attack for Teachers.* Columbus: Charles Merrill, 1974.

*Student materials:*

> Bassano, Sharron. *Consonants Sound Easy!* San Francisco: The Alemany Press, 1980.
>
> Bassano, Sharron. *Sounds Easy! A Phonics Workbook for Beginning E.S.L. Students.* San Francisco: The Alemany Press, 1980.
>
> Boning, Richard A. *Specific Skill Series.* Baldwin, NY: Barnell Loft, 1973.
>
> Boning, Richard A. *Supportive Reading Skills.* Baldwin, NY: Dexter & Westbrook, 1974.

# BACKGROUND FOR WORD RECOGNITION

To use word recognition strategies, the learner needs certain specific language skills. As readers process written language, their understanding of earlier words in sentences and their knowledge of syntax helps them continually anticipate succeeding words. Such use of context requires a good oral vocabulary and the knowledge of, or at least a feeling for, common syntactical and semantic language clues. Using their oral language background, beginning readers can frequently identify unfamiliar words by using only sentence context clues. Phonetic analysis, on the other hand, requires the ability to discriminate speech sounds from one another and match various letters or groups of letters with the sounds they represent. Also needed is the ability to blend individual sounds to approximate a word's pronunciation. A good oral vocabulary is needed since it usually does very little good to sound out a word if, upon doing so, the word is still unfamiliar. Structural analysis also requires a well-established oral vocabulary as well as knowledge of common roots and affixes and a sense of syllabication.

The following chart compares native English-speaking students with ESL students in terms of their background knowledge of these specific language skills.

| Language skill | English-speaking student | ESL student |
| --- | --- | --- |
| Oral/aural vocabulary | Has acquired wide oral/aural English vocabulary | Is acquiring English oral/aural vocabulary; number of familiar words is limited |
| Auditory discrimination | Has heard English speech sounds since birth; has learned to discriminate these from one another | Is beginning to hear and discriminate English speech sounds; may not hear some sounds at all or may confuse some sounds with others; is still learning to distinguish English sounds |
| Production of speech sounds | Can produce English speech sounds | Is beginning to produce English speech sounds; may have difficulty producing some sounds that are not of native language |
| Knowledge of English syntax | Knows English syntax; has been hearing and forming English sentences since learning to talk | Is learning English syntax; often makes oral syntactical errors |
| Knowledge of syllabication principles | Is generally familiar with English syllables orally; can hear distinct syllables in English words or can learn to hear these rather easily | Is acquiring English oral/aural vocabulary; often cannot hear separate syllables in English words and often does not pronounce all syllables in all English words. |

While the native English speaker has a rich background of specific language skills to use in acquiring word recognition skills, the ESL student is limited, not only in general English facility but also in specific language skills needed to acquire word recognition strategies for figuring out English words.

Because ESL students lack these specific language skills, it follows that their instruction in word recognition needs to be different from that designed for English-speaking students. ESL students need to learn the basic skills of word recognition. Their instructional programs need to be geared to specific needs and sensitive to specific limitations. With these ideas in mind, we suggest a way of designing word recognition instruction appropriate for the ESL student.

## WORD RECOGNITION INSTRUCTION FOR ESL STUDENTS

### Using Context Clues

Context clues (surrounding words, language patterns, and pictures or other graphic aids) are some of the most powerful word recognition tools available to the reader. Using context allows the reader to reduce uncertainty about the unknown word and to identify it more easily. To illustrate, we will simulate your encounter of an unknown word in print by using a nonsensical combination of letters to represent a word you know orally. Imagine that you encounter this word alone:

mxb

The word is meaningless at this point, but as we add sentence context gradually, the meaning will become more and more clear:

a mxb

a mxb flies

A mxb flies in the air and carries passengers.

Partial context (a mxb, a mxb flies) allows you to reduce uncertainty about the unknown word; it is a noun and it cound be kite, bird, or plane. It is almost certainly not tree, house, or any number of other words. The full context allows you to eliminate some choices and settle on plane as the almost certain one. (Other choices are possible, of course; mxb could be blimp, helicopter, or other such words for passenger carriers. To be certain, you need to see the actual word in print so as to note the particular letter combination.)

Context clues are extremely useful tools. Unique considerations arise in teaching ESL students to use English context clues. Effective use of context in any language derives largely from the reader's experience with that language and culture. For example, the reader from a Judeo-

Christian culture will probably be better able to use context clues to identify the last word in the sentence *The teacher had the patience of Job* than will a student from a different cultural background (Saville-Troike, 1976). Students who are acquainted with the story of Job will likely have heard the term "the patience of Job" so that the word *Job* can be rather easily identified and will not be mistaken for the word that means an occupation. The particular context clues of this sentence are cultural. The "in text" context clues are not useful to the student from a non-Judeo-Christian background. Similarly, references to Thanksgiving turkey, Fourth of July fireworks, and other typically American language/cultural phenomena will not be a part of most ESL students' backgrounds and therefore will be of limited use as contextural aids when those students are reading. A sentence or paragraph which supplies sufficient context clues for the typical English-speaking student may not be as helpful to the newcomer ESL student. Also, what may be helpful to one student may not be to another because of possible wide differences in students' backgrounds.

ESL students practice using context clues as they gradually master the ability to handle oral English. As they develop oral sentence sense for the English language, coming to recognize common patterns and contexts, they will build their ability to use a similar sense of context in reading language. Direct instruction in the use of context clues is essential for these students, and particular attention must be paid to helping them employ context clues that are useful. With these general ideas in mind, we suggest some strategies for students at each stage.

### Stage 1 Students

With the emphasis on oral language development, instruction should focus on helping students develop a sense for which language patterns sound "right" orally. Informal conversations build a general sense of how words are ordered in English, the basic knowledge that leads to successful use of context clues to derive meaning. The same instructional activities used to develop oral vocabulary will also build skill in using context clues orally. For example, those activities which focus on repetitious patterns of language will develop understanding of specific word patterns. Stories read aloud or told will also develop this understanding. As students participate in these activities, additional practice in using context clues may be accomplished with these kinds of activities:

1. Read students a poem with a refrain. After they have heard the refrain several times, read the first part and have students complete the refrain orally.
2. Play "missing word" games in which students supply one or two words orally for statements read aloud. Use familiar statements,

such as those in students' dictated pattern stories, to make the activity easy.

*Stage 2 Students*

As students begin dictating stories, they will create reading materials with highly meaningful contexts, maximizing their chances for successfully using context clues to identify those words which are unfamiliar in print. As students become more comfortable reading their stories, these activities will give them specific practice in using reading context clues:

1. Give students a copy of a previously dictated story from which several key words have been omitted. Have students read the story silently to determine what the missing words are. Answers may be supplied in scrambled order at the bottom of the page to make the task easier. (See Figure 4-G on page 54.)
2. Give students teacher-written passages using words students have used in dictated stories. Include one or two "new" words (unknown to students) that can be identified by using context clues. Have students read the passages silently and figure out the unknown words.
3. As students reread dictated stories and come to an unknown word, show them how to skip the word momentarily and read on to develop the full context in which the word appears. Simply reading to the end of a sentence will often enable students to go back and identify the unknown word.

*Stage 3 Students*

Stage 3 students should continue Stage 2 context clue activities and may also be given the same kinds of activities using other-author materials. They may also be introduced to the various types of context clues that are available to readers. The list below, adapted from Roe, *et al.* (1978), illustrates this variety.

| Type of Context Clue | Example |
| --- | --- |
| 1. Definition | A *wind tunnel* is a machine used to control wind speeds for scientific experiments. |
| 2. Restatement | The mother kangaroo has a *pouch*, or bag, on the front of her body for carrying baby kangaroos. |
| 3. Example | "Go to your room!" is an example of a *command.* |
| 4. Comparison/Contrast | A *sieve,* like a filter, can strain liquids. In winter bears *hibernate;* in summer they are awake and moving about. |

| | |
|---|---|
| 5. Description | A *raccoon* is a small, furry animal with a striped tail and markings on its face that look like a mask. |
| 6. Synonyms/Antonyms | The *trolley,* or streetcar, carried many passengers in the city. It was a *steaming* day; rain in the evening made it cooler. |
| 7. Association | She was as *protective* of her children as a mother tiger is of her cubs. |
| 8. Reflection of Mood | Sarah saw the rattlesnake move closer. She knew it was poisonous, and it seemed about ready to attack. Sarah was *terrified.* |
| 9. Summary | He knew his products well and could talk about them easily. He saw many customers and made many sales. He was a very *capable* salesman. |

As these clues appear in students' reading materials, time should be spent discussing how to use them. Exercises may also be specifically designed to give practice with these various types of context clues.

## *Using Phonetic Analysis*

It can be useful to be able to "sound out" unfamiliar words in print, so phonetic analysis (phonics) can be considered an essential skill for the ESL student, just as it is for the native English reader. However, it is also an area of instruction laden with problems. In order to learn sound/letter associations, one must be able first to discriminate sounds aurally and then must learn to associate those sounds with the letters that represent them. Successful application of phonics is dependent on the reader's ability to hear and produce the sounds of the language. Lack of experience with English sounds and patterns may make the ESL student unable to recognize, discriminate, and use those sounds in speech. This inability, in turn, can make it difficult for the student to sound out words in print. Table 5-1 identifies some of the sounds which may cause problems for students from various language backgrounds.

*Table 5-1*

**A SELECTED LIST OF PRONUNCIATION/AURAL DISCRIMINATION PROBLEMS FOR ALL/MOST LEARNERS OF ENGLISH**

| Problems for | Areas of difficulty |
|---|---|
| all students | /dh/-/th/<br>/r/<br>/S/, /ED/<br>"relaxed" pronunciation |

most students                    final /b/, /d/, /g/, /p/, /t/, /k/
                                 /d/-/t/
                                 /ŋ/
                                 /z/-/s/
                                 /l/-/r/
                                 /v/-/w/
                                 /ch/-/sh/
                                 /y/-/j/
                                 consonant clusters


## A SELECTED LIST OF PRONUNCIATION/AURAL DISCRIMINATION PROBLEMS ACCORDING TO STUDENT'S NATIVE LANGUAGE

| Problems for speakers of | Areas of difficulty |
|---|---|
| Arabic | /b/-/p/<br>/ŋ/<br>/sh/-/j/-/zh/<br>/g/-/j/<br>consonant clusters |
| Burmese | final /b/, /d/, /g/, /p/, /t/, /k/<br>/v/-/f/<br>/l/-/r/<br>consonant clusters |
| Chinese | /b/, /d/, /g/<br>/v/<br>/dh/-/th/<br>final consonants except /n/, /ŋ/<br>/sh/-/ch/ |
| French | /dh/-/th/<br>/h/<br>/s/-/t/-/th/<br>/ch/-/sh/ |
| German | /b/-/p/<br>/n/-/ŋ/<br>/dh/-/th/<br>/z/-/s/<br>/v/-/w/<br>/t/-/th/<br>/d/-/dh/<br>/ch/-/sh/<br>/y/-/j/<br>voiced final consonants |

| Problems for speakers of | Areas of difficulty |
|---|---|
| Greek | /n/-/ŋ/<br>/z/-/s/<br>/w/, /hw/<br>/b/-/v/<br>/s/-/sh/<br>/z/-/dh/<br>/ch/-/sh/<br>/y/-/j/ |
| Haitian Creole | same as French plus final consonants |
| Indonesian | /v/-/f/<br>/dh/-/th/<br>/zh/-/sh/<br>/v/-/w/<br>consonant clusters<br>final /b/, /d/, /g/, /z/, /j/ |
| Farsi (Persian) | /ŋ/<br>/v/-/w/<br>/th/-/s/<br>consonant clusters |
| Italian | /dh/-/th/<br>/h/<br>/s/-/sh/<br>consonant clusters |
| Japanese | /dh/-/th/<br>/l/-/r/<br>/v/-/w/<br>/s/-/sh/<br>/ch/-/sh/<br>consonant clusters |
| Korean | /b/-/p/<br>/d/-/t/<br>/g/-/k/<br>/dh/-/th/<br>/j/-/ch/<br>/l/-/r/<br>all voiced consonants |
| Laotian | same as Thai, but not /l/-/r/ |

| Problems for speakers of | Areas of difficulty |
|---|---|
| Navajo | /b/-/p/<br>/m/-/n/-/ŋ/<br>/v/-/f/<br>/dh/-/th/<br>/p/-/f/<br>/b/-/v/<br>/f/-/s/<br>/th/-/s/<br>/th/-/t/<br>/d/-/dh/<br>/z/-/dh/ |
| Polish | /ŋ/<br>/dh/-/th/<br>/l/<br>/w/ |
| Portugese | final /b/, /d/, /g/, /p/, /t/, /k/<br>/n/, /ŋ/<br>/j/-/ch/<br>final /l/<br>/h/<br>consonant clusters |
| Russian | /m/-/n/-/ŋ/<br>/dh/-/th/<br>/j/-/ch/<br>/h/-/hw/-/w/<br>/f/-/th/<br>/th/-/s/<br>/th/-/t/<br>/d/-/dh/<br>/z/-/dh/<br>all voiced final consonants |
| Spanish | /d/<br>/m/-/n/-/ŋ/<br>/z/-/s/<br>/b/-/v/<br>/th/-/s/<br>/s/-/sh/-/ch/<br>/y/-/j/<br>consonant clusters<br>final voiced consonants |

| Problems for speakers of | Areas of difficulty |
|---|---|
| Thai | final /b/, /d/, /g/<br>/dh/-/th/<br>/z/-/s/<br>/j/-/ch/<br>/l/-/r/<br>/v/-/w/<br>/ch/-/sh/ |
| Turkish | /g/-/k/<br>/ŋ/<br>/v/-/w/<br>consonant clusters<br>final voiced consonants |
| Vietnamese | /p/<br>/k/<br>/ŋ/<br>/zh/-/sh/<br>/r/<br>/y/<br>final voiced consonants |

*From Edith Crowell Trager,* PD's in depth: Pronunciation/ Aural Discrimination Drills for Learners of English, *Culver City, CA: ELS Publications, 1982, xvi-xxi.*

Each student will have unique difficulties with the English sound system. Knowing the sounds that are most difficult for the student will come from an understanding of the student's native language as it compares with English and also from observing the student's pronunciation problems in English.

Because of these difficulties, phonics instruction for ESL students should be carried out in the context of whole, known words as opposed to isolated sounds. The goal of instruction should be to help students learn to associate letters or letter combinations with the sounds they represent. Using known words allows students to learn associations in a meaningful context, increasing the students' chances for success. Emphasis should be placed first on words containing sounds which students can discriminate auditorially and which they use easily in speech. Once sound/letter associations are learned for these, the more difficult sounds may be introduced.

When planning a phonics program, it is also helpful to be aware of the demands various activities place on students. Phonics activities fall into four basic categories. These are:

1. Auditory-Auditory. Both the stimulus and the response are oral.

For example:

> Teacher: Do cat and city start with the same sound?
> Student: No.
> Teacher: Do cat and kitty start with the same sound?
> Student: Yes.

2. Auditory-Visual. The stimulus is oral, but the student selects or produces a response in printed form. For example:

> Teacher: Write a word which starts with the same sound as cat.
> Student: (Writes kite. Writes car.)

3. Visual-Auditory. The stimulus is presented in print, but the student response is oral. For example:

> Teacher: Look at these words. Which ones start with the same sound?
> (city sit kite)
> Student: City and sit start with the same sound.

4. Visual-Visual. Both stimulus and response are in print. For example:

> Teacher: Look at this word. Write a word that starts with the same sound.
> Student: (Reads cat and writes kite.)

Recognizing the specific requirements of each activity will help to pinpoint where students may be having trouble.

Activities may also be categorized on a second dimension — whether the response requires the student simply to choose an answer or to produce an answer independently. For example, "Choose a word that starts with the same sound as cat" requires only a choice, while "Write a word that begins with the same sound as cat" requires production of an answer. Usually, choice activities will be easier than production activities. Here are examples of choice and production activities to develop sound/letter associations. Each activity is designed to develop awareness of beginning sounds and can be adapted for work with final sounds or sounds in medial positions.

*Choice Activities*

1. Auditory-Auditory. Compile a list of pairs of words that are aurally familiar to students. In some pairs beginning sounds should be the same (book/bat); in other pairs these sounds should be different (best/car). Say each pair to students and have them tell whether or not the words begin with the same sound.

2. Auditory-Visual. Compile a list of words that are aurally familiar to students. Give students word cards that begin with the same sounds as the words on the list. (These words should also be familiar to students.)

Pronounce the list words one at a time and have students select words from their cards that begin with the same sounds.

3. Visual-Auditory. Put three or four words on the board that are familiar to students. Tell students to examine the words and choose and read aloud the ones that begin with the same sound.

4. Visual-Visual. Put one or two words on the board that are familiar to students. Have them look through their Word Banks for words that begin with the same sounds.

*Production Activities*

1. Auditory-Auditory. Compile a list of words that are aurally familiar to students. Pronounce these words one at a time, and have students respond with words that start with the same sounds. Reinforce correct responses by having students say both words again, listening for the same sound at the beginning.

2. Auditory-Visual. Compile a list of words that are aurally familiar to students. Pronounce these words one at a time, and have students write words that begin with the same sounds.

3. Visual-Auditory. Put several words on the board that are familiar to students. Have them say words that begin with the same sounds.

4. Visual-Visual. Put several words on the board that are familiar to students. Have them write words that begin with the same sounds.

Both choice and production activities can be used with students at all three stages. However, at each stage certain emphases will be more important than others. Here are some things to consider for each stage.

It is most important for stage 1 students to learn to communicate in English. Phonics instruction should be given a very small time allotment in the overall Stage 1 program. When students are able to communicate fairly well in English and are learning to recognize some key words in print, some phonics activities may be introduced. Phonics instruction at this stage should focus on discrimination/recognition of sounds which are common to English and the student's native language. Only known words, for example, key vocabulary words, should be used for this instruction.

Stage 2 students will be dictating stories, and phonics activities may increase somewhat for these learners, using words that are familiar to students in printed form. As students make progress learning sound/letter associations for sounds that are common to English and their native language, some unfamiliar sounds may be introduced, but the major emphasis should be on learning sound/letter associations for sounds that are already familiar.

Stage 3 students, with their greater mastery of English, will be able to handle a greater number and variety of phonics activities. As students demonstrate mastery of a number of sound/letter associations, emphasis may be placed on work with those sounds which are not part of the student's native language sound system. Students should not be expected to learn to pronounce these sounds accurately at first; it may take some students several years to master a speech sound which does not occur in their native language. However, students should be helped to recognize those sounds when they hear them and to learn which letters represent those sounds in print.

Students should be helped to develop alphabetized pronunciation keys, using known words from dictated stories to illustrate the various sounds of English. These keys will be useful as a reference for students; if students encounter unfamiliar words in print and are not sure how to sound them out, they can turn to their pronunciation keys and find known words that illustrate the sounds. Because of the great variety of letters that represent English vowels, a pronunciation key will be most useful as a reference for vowel sounds. Pronunciation keys should be developed gradually, as students begin to work with sound/letter associations and use words naturally in their dictated stories that illustrate the various sounds they are working on.

Despite the importance of phonics for word recognition, students should not come to rely on sounding out words as their only strategy for identifying unknown words. As students make progress learning sound/letter associations, they should be given opportunities to use phonics in conjunction with other word recognition skills, especially context clues. Flexible use of the two strategies will make for more effective and efficient word recognition. To help students use both skills together, activities such as this one should be assigned:

> Give students teacher-written passages (or short passages from easy-to-read books) from which some words have been omitted and replaced with the first letters of those words. For example,
>
> Yesterday I took my d＿＿＿＿ for a walk. We walked and walked, and then we came h＿＿＿＿ . We had a good t＿＿＿＿ .
>
> Have students read the passages silently and, using the first letter and context clues, try to figure out the missing word. Use passages with known words and reasonable context clues to make the task easy to do.

## Using Structural Analysis

Structural analysis (dividing words into syllables and into roots and affixes) is also an essential word recognition strategy. The key aspect of structural analysis, correct syllable identification, might be difficult for students since it is largely dependent on the ability to hear the syllables correctly in spoken English. Just as discriminating unfamiliar sounds of

English is hard, discriminating individual syllables is also troublesome.

Some rules (for example, syllables are usually divided between double consonants) may prove useful tools if they are taught using known words and if they are used in conjunction with oral language training. That is, as students learn to pronounce English syllables more accurately, it is useful for them to see how the printed word is divided into syllables. However, students must also be made aware that the rules alone will not help them identify unfamiliar words; dividing words into syllables is usually only a way of breaking words into manageable parts. The words must still be sounded out, and the context must still be considered to determine the pronunciation and meaning of a word. Thus, syllabication rules are useful to some extent but should not be given major emphasis in the ESL instructional program.

The second aspect of structural analysis, the ability to divide words into their *roots* and *affixes,* may be more useful to the ESL student since this ability has the potential to increase the student's vocabulary geometrically. As students come to recognize common affixes (*pre-, inter-, trans-,* for example) they will be better able to identify unfamiliar words containing those parts.

It is best to teach structural analysis using a guided discovery approach rather than a rote drill approach. Guided discovery learning, an inductive approach, involves the use of teacher questions to help the student discover patterns in a series of known words. For example, students can be asked to look for and discuss patterns in groups of words such as:

| | | |
|---|---|---|
| hitting | tapping | funnier |
| sitting | easier | choosier |
| running | happier | |

Teacher questions might include: What are the root words? How are the endings added? What is the pattern? This approach is preferable because the emphasis is placed on studying the words, not simply on memorizing rules which may not be meaningful to the students.

With these ideas in mind, we propose several activities for students at each of the three stages.

The major emphasis for Stage 1 students should be building oral/aural awareness of syllables and accents in English. Much of this emphasis will occur naturally as students learn to speak English and refine their pronunciation skills. Specific practice may be given with activities like this:

> Present orally several known multi-syllable words. Tell students how many syllables each word has and illustrate by exaggerating the pronunciation of the syllables. Have students repeat, listening for the number of syllables. Then present other multi-syllable words and have students tell how many syllables they hear.

Stage 2 students can be made aware of syllables as they occur in words they use in their dictated stories. These activities will be useful at this stage:

1. Give students small cards on which have been printed separate parts of various known compound words. Have them put the cards together to make the familiar words. Cards may be cut like puzzle pieces so that matching the proper parts will be that much easier.

2. Find singular and plural forms in students' dictated stories to illustrate how words change from the singular to the plural. Then show students unknown plural forms for which the singulars are known. Have students identify these new words by using their knowledge of the singulars.

3. Using words from dictated stories, show students several words that follow a given syllable pattern. Show them how the words are divided into syllables and have them figure out the rule that has been followed.

Stage 3 students may be asked to apply syllabication rules to figure out unknown words in dictated stories and other reading materials. They should be helped to divide the words into syllables and then sound them out. These students may also work with common roots and affixes so as to learn to apply this knowledge to unknown words which contain these elements. These activities are typical of those that most Stage 3 students can handle:

1. Compile a list of words containing a common root or affix, such as tele- (television, telephone). Choose words that the student has used in dictated stories or familiar words from other reading materials. Discuss the meaning of the element, showing the student how the element affects the meaning of the words on the list. Then give students one or two unfamiliar words, in sentence or paragraph context, that contain the same element. Help the student apply knowledege of the element's meaning to figuring out the unknown words.

2. Compile a new list of words that use a common element. For example, if the student is learning tele- as in television and telephone, introduce telegraph or teleprompter. Put these words in sentences and have students use context clues and knowledge of the element's meaning to figure out the new words. (This activity should only be done when students have already learned the meaning of the element that is used.)

## *SOME FINAL THOUGHTS ON WORD RECOGNITION*

A good word recognition program will provide a balance of various activities for using context clues, applying phonics, and using structural analysis to figure out unknown words. Students should also be helped to use these skills together. For example, they should see that dividing a word into syllables will make it easier to sound out, and the sentence (or paragraph) context will help to determine pronunciation and meaning. Phonics exercises or syllabication exercises alone will not help students develop effective word recognition strategies. Also, ESL students will usually not learn these skills as successfully by using materials that are designed for native English-speaking students. The best progam will develop skills within a meaningful context such as LEA dictated stories.

Finally, a variety of activities should be included in the program. Students who have difficulty with one type of exercise may find another, designed to develop the same skill, easier to handle. By trying different activities and noting student response and progress, the program can be modified to provide the best combination of lessons. We have suggested only a few basic activities that work well with many ESL students of all ages. Consult the sources listed on page 66 for more ideas. Although some of these sources are intended for the native English-speaking student, the ideas can be modified to suit the ESL student, using the principles we have outlined in this chapter.

## *SUMMARY*

Students need to learn to use context clues, phonics, and structural analysis to develop word recognition skills. Stage 1 instruction focuses on oral context, auditory discrimination of English sounds, and oral/aural awareness of syllables. Stage 2 instruction introduces these skills as they apply to written English. Stage 3 instruction refines and extends skill learning in each area. Word recognition lessons should supplement the basic program of discussion and dictation and should be planned to tie in directly with the words and sentences students use in their dictation.

## *REFERENCES*

Roe, B. D., Stoodt, B. D., & Burns, P. C. *Reading Instruction in the Secondary School.* Chicago: Rand McNally, 1978.

Saville-Troike, M. *Foundations for Teaching English as a Second Language: Theory and Method.* Englewood Cliffs, NJ: Prentice Hall, 1976.

Trager, E. C. *PD's in Depth: Pronunciation/Aural Discrimination Drills for Learners of English.* Culver City, CA: ELS Publications, 1982, xvi-xxi.

# Chapter 6

# Student Writing

It is generally accepted that writing is more difficult than listening, speaking, or reading. Producing meaning through writing requires more effort than recognizing meaning through listening or reading. What can be said aloud cannot be expressed as easily or quickly in writing; besides deciding what to say, the writer must follow the conventions of spelling and punctuation that will make the message understandable to others. Also, while a speaker can use gestures, the listener's reactions, and other face-to-face communication aids, a writer must work harder to express meaning to an unseen audience. Usually students develop writing abilities in school after oral language and reading abilities are rather well established.

Learning the skills of written expression can be difficult for ESL students, who must learn to write a language which is orally unfamiliar. In addition to the difficulties inherent in trying to translate oral speech into written language, the physical aspects of writing also may pose problems for many students. Kindergarten and first grade pupils typically write with difficulty because they are just learning to hold pencils and form letters and words. Likewise, very young ESL pupils or older students who have not already learned to write in their native language are faced with the demanding task of developing sufficient eye-hand coordination while struggling to remember and negotiate correctly the complexities of written English.

Recent renewed interest in helping students write better and more easily has produced many books and articles outlining models of the writing process and suggesting how to organize instruction. Moffett (1968, 1981), Britton (1970), and Myers (1980) are among those who offer both theoretical and practical views on the writing process. These materials, presented with the native English-speaking student in mind, assume mastery of oral English as well as acquisition of reading skills.

The emphasis is on structuring programs and assigning activities that will help students use their highly familiar language to express their ideas in writing. While these sources provide excellent background for understanding the writing process and making some decisions about instruction, their procedures must usually be modified to suit the particular needs of the ESL student.

A successful ESL writing program, like oral language and reading programs, emphasizes the immediate relevance and utility of writing as well as introduces specific skills consistent with the oral language proficiency and reading ability acquired by the students. Generally accepted views on the teaching of writing can be combined with the basic philosophy of LEA to design meaningful and appropriate activities for these students. We will suggest some ways to design writing acquisition activities.

## THE COMPOSING PROCESS

The composing process includes four steps: prewriting, writing, revising, and rewriting. Each step must be viewed in light of the special needs of ESL students.

### *Prewriting*

Prewriting is the time spent developing ideas before making an attempt to put them on paper formally. The prewriting step parallels "discussion before dictation." At this point, the student has an opportunity not only to generate ideas but also to review vocabulary and language patterns before attempting to use those same elements in written language, just as the student phrases ideas during discussion before dictating a story.

Prewriting language review should be accomplished through meaningful activities such as:

1. *Guided listening.* Students listen for certain kinds of language while a selection is read or told, e.g., all the words the author uses to describe a snow storm. More advanced students may write brief notes on the target items. Discussion following listening allows students to compare what they heard and present opinions about the effectiveness of the author's choices.

2. *Guided imagining.* Like guided listening, guided imagining requires students to focus attention on certain words and ideas; however, students compose most of the details rather than just listen for them. For example, the teacher may say, "You are walking along a path. Think about how the path looks. How wide is it? Is it rough or smooth? Where is it going? What can you see in

the distance?" Students may share their imaginings, expressing the thoughts and feelings the experience evoked. (See "Guided Fantasy" in Bassano and Christison, 1981.)

3. *Clustering.* Clustering is one way to organize ideas. Students individually or in groups think of and arrange related words and phrases graphically around a key concept. Clustering allows students to organize thoughts and achieve new insights without fear of making mistakes. A cluster can never be wrong since it represents the student's own perceptions. Once the cluster has been completed, the resulting graphic figure serves much the same purpose as an outline in helping the writer to organize and remember key words and ideas. Figure 6-A illustrates one prewriting cluster done by an ESL student and the composition that was done based on the cluster. (Also see Hanf, 1971, and Rico, and Claggett, 1980.)

*Figure 6-A*

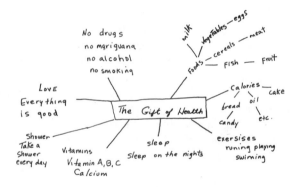

Good health is very important to me because having a good health we can live many years. We have to eat good food with vitamins and calcium too. We take care off our health because if we don't we can have many problems with our body. Doing exercise is good too because we need that for our body. If people eat some thing that have calories is not good. The drugs are bad thing for our body. Same people that like drugs they did because they sometimes drink alcohol and smoke mariguana those things are very bad. People have to stop doing that If people stop smoking and drinking they are going to have a good health like us.

Other kinds of meaningful prewriting activities can be helpful. Brainstorming, free discussion, or recording thoughts on tape are among the possibilities. Any prewriting activity that assists the writer in organizing thoughts, reviewing relevant vocabulary, and establishing the focus for writing is good. (See Christison and Bassano, 1981 and Christison, 1982 for other prewriting ideas.)

### *Writing*

The first writing step is actually a beginning rather than the end of the composing process. This is "getting it down" in rough form — the ideas stimulated by the prewriting activity. It is not a time to worry about correct form, spelling, or other mechanical elements. Students need to write their first thoughts, knowing that these efforts will not be evaluated or criticized. Errors in language usage or mechanics should be ignored at this point. Error correction can interfere with acquisition. Students should write without feeling self-conscious or inadequate.

### *Revising*

Many times writing programs focus on revision but inappropriately emphasize correcting mechanical errors. Writing mechanics (spelling, punctuation, usage) should be handled only after issues such as clarity of meaning and successful completion of purpose have been dealt with *and* only after the writer is able to write comfortably and fluently on a wide range of topics. Correcting mechanical errors must be presented as an aid to improving communication rather than as an end in itself.

Writing is emphasized as an act of communication when a clear audience is provided for help with revision. Students should be given many opportunities to share and discuss their writing with other students and to hear and react to what peers have written. These sessions help students identify aspects of their writing which are particularly effective as well as those which need further work.

### *Rewriting*

The final step, rewriting, is just that, a *new* writing, not just a copying over in ink. Rewriting is the time for incorporating suggestions from peers and for producing a final copy. At this point students should be urged to produce their best possible work, the most effective and correct that they can manage.

Writing lessons need not always include all four steps of the composing process. Some assignments, for example, may involve only a brief prewriting discussion and production of an unrefined writing sample with no revision or rewriting expected. Also, these four steps do not need equal emphasis for students at different stages. Planning an effective writing program requires an understanding of the totality of the composing process and of the function served by each step. We have only presented the outline of the process to provide a framework for the writing activities we recommend for each stage. For further, specific reading on the various elements of the composing process, we particularly recommend the sources cited earlier as well as Elbow (1973), Martin, *et al.* (1976), and Caplan and Keech (1980).

## TEACHING WRITING: GENERAL PRINCIPLES

As most ESL students have not fully mastered English oral language and reading skills, it is especially important that their writing reinforce and extend language learning in these areas. In an LEA program, dictation, one form of composing, provides a first step to mastering written composition as the students learn to read. Writing becomes a natural extension of dictating/reading but does not replace dictation. Dictation allows students to make full use of their growing oral English, including words which they cannot yet read. Writing allows the student to use the same language, but because of the additional demands associated with writing, most students will choose to write primarily words which they are already able to read. It is easier to write words whose forms are familiar, having been seen often in print. For full development of language skills, dictation and writing are both necessary parts of the instructional program. Reading written work aloud and hearing others' work also reinforces reading and oral language skills as well as helps students revise their work. Sharing sessions, whether or not actual revisions are made in writing, are important to demonstrate writing-as-communication as well as to develop the other language skills.

Students' ages, backgrounds, and abilities will suggest when to introduce which writing activities. Students with experience writing a native language will generally be able to begin writing in English sooner and more easily than those with little or no other writing experience. Students whose native languages are written with the Roman alphabet will also have an easier time writing English than will those from, for example, China, Japan, or Saudi Arabia.* General ability to master speaking and reading English also influences writing readiness. As a rule, students at each stage will be able to handle some forms of writing as long as they have acquired some oral and reading English vocabulary and they are able to form English letters with consistency and ease.

Handwriting instruction, using any systematic program, will have to precede composition instruction for those who have not learned to form

*Seward (1982) may be a helpful workbook for "non-Roman alphabet" students. This is a penmanship practice book that presents letters in families rather than A to Z.

the letters of the English alphabet. We recommend beginning handwriting instruction with Stage 1 students after they have had much oral language practice and have learned to recognize a few English words. Instruction at this time should focus on writing a few known words, including the student's name, and on practicing letter formation. Instruction should be introduced or continued at later stages depending on need.

These general principles should guide the planning of basic writing activities:

1. Base student writing on personally *meaningful* topics. Just as dictation is based on relevant, experience-based topics, writing also should stem from what is of interest and familiar to the student.

2. Have talk precede writing. Because writing is more difficult than dictating, students should be given many prewriting opportunities to review orally what they want to say in writing.

3. Emphasize the act of composing. Present writing as a form of communication, not a series of drills.

4. Avoid error correction. Recognize errors in usage, awkward phrasing, and difficulties with mechanics as natural outcomes of limited mastery of English. Handle errors very sensitively and only after the student is able to write comfortably and fluently.

5. Relate writing assignments to reading and oral language activities. At first, writing should be directly related to dictated stories. As students are later exposed to a greater variety of reading material, the additional models of English can be used to refine written expression and broaden the content of written work.

These general principles should be followed when using the specific plans we suggest for students at each stage.

## WRITING FOR STAGE 1 STUDENTS

Stage 1 students should be allowed to acquire writing skills at a comfortable pace. Most, still mastering oral language and reading skills in English, will not be able to write easily at first. They will need introductory, simple, composing activities that can help them get started without frustration. Here are some easy activities that focus on using known words. While actual writing is limited, composing meaningful statements is emphasized.

1. Encourage students to practice handwriting skills by copying key words into picture dictionaries or onto a second set of word cards. Meaning is the main emphasis at this point since the words were originally selected by the student.

2. As the student moves into dictating pattern stories, leave a blank

page opposite each dictated line so that the student may copy the sentence and illustrate it a second time. Figure 6-B illustrates one such page from a pattern story book.

*Figure 6-B*

Figure 6-C illustrates another way of using pattern stories.

*Figure 6-C*

After a group discussion of the pattern story *The Farmer and the Skunk* (see page 26) and dictating a farmer and skunk story, Natsumi wrote a story, following the same pattern, about a skunk named Bingy and her friend named Natsumi.

3. Give students envelopes containing collections of known words that make meaningful sentences. Have them arrange the words to make sentences.

4. Have students choose several words from their Word Banks and arrange them to form sentences. Give them any new word cards they may need to complete the sentences.

5. Have students listen to or read a familiar story with some words and/or phrases omitted. Have them select word cards from their Word Banks to fill in the blanks.

Mechanically correct writing should never be a goal for Stage 1 students. Students who choose to correct their spelling or other mechanical elements may be helped in doing so, but the major purpose for writing at this stage is to increase the quantity of written language until the student feels comfortable and secure producing it. The output is in many ways "pre-production" output and focuses on meaningful input prior to polished production. The most important steps for these students are prewriting and writing; revising and rewriting are not emphasized in these initial activities. This is an acquisition stage when we present as many building blocks as possible. More polished production will emerge later.

## WRITING FOR STAGE 2 STUDENTS

As the student moves from dictation of single words and repetitive simple sentences into more complete language usage, writing lessons reflect that change by introducing gradually more challenging tasks. These activities, for example, require somewhat more writing but are still based on dictated stories and known story words:

1. Give students previously dictated stories, cut up into sentence strips. Have them arrange the strips in order to reform the story.

2. Give students four or five sentence strips from a story they have not seen before but which includes mostly known words. (Make up the story or choose one that was dictated by other students.) Have students arrange these sentence strips in order to form a story.

3. Arrange known dictated story words in columns according to function in sentences. Have students choose a word or phrase from each column to compose a sentence, making as many different sentences as they can. For example,

| The | car | ran | under the tree |
| A | dog | was | through the window |
| An | apple | stopped | on the chair |
| | man | flew | in the street |
| | bird | sat | |

4. Have students dictate the first part of a story. After three or four sentences have been dictated, give students the story to complete independently in writing. (Stage 1 students should complete the story orally.)

5. Have students review previously dictated stories and make additions in writing.

6. Have students choose several favorite words from their Word Banks. Have them discuss the memories and associations the words evoke and then write these ideas.

Once students make progress with these activities, they can be encouraged to write more complete stories. Figure 6-D shows a full story written by a Stage 2 student. This writing followed a discussion between student and teacher which reviewed details about the student's recent vacation. Much more was discussed than is reflected in the story. Also, typically, the child's oral language was more varied in vocabulary and language structures than the story suggests, but the piece reveals a clear sense of communicating about the people and events closest to the child's life.

*Figure 6-D*

> my vacation
>
> On my vacation I went to take care of son japonese children. They have nine puppies. and one day one puppy gies Because my sister's babi carry to much the puppy.
> and I went to Carpinteria to the Church.

As students are able to write simple stories and accounts, a broader range of activities may be introduced to refine their skills. These activities are particularly suitable for the Stage 2 student as they all grow directly from oral language activities. They emphasize meaningful use of English for a variety of purposes.

1. Have a discussion about what is going on in the classroom that day. For example, talk about who is present and absent, how people are dressed, what the class accomplished earlier in the day, or what may be seen from the window. Ask students to write a brief

description incorporating their observations.

2. Ask students to tell about their usual routines as they prepare for school and then make the trip. Then have them write their reports.

3. Give students copies of cartoons from which the characters' dialogue has been omitted. Have them compose orally, experimenting with various things the characters might be saying, and then write their ideas on the cartoons. (Also see Christison and Bassano, 1981.)

4. Give students magazine illustrations and discuss with them various features of the pictures. Have them write a few statements to describe the pictures.

5. Have students invent and act out brief social exchanges, for example, asking directions, making a purchase in a store, greeting someone on the street, or ordering food at a snack bar. Have them write these in dialogue form.

6. Read aloud or tell interesting stories to students. Have them discuss characters and events and perhaps act out one or two scenes. Then have students summarize the stories in their own words in writing. (Also see Dennis, et. al., 1981.)

7. Encourage students to keep journals. Begin by having students discuss daily school activities and dictate a class journal to record daily events. Then have students keep individual journals to record events at home and at school. (Olsen, 1977; Christison and Bassano, 1981.)

8. Explain the concept of autobiography to students, perhaps reading portions of an autobiography to illustrate. Have them discuss their own personal histories and then write sketches of their own lives. (Riverol, 1984.)

9. Read a story aloud to the group and discuss favorite elements of the tale. Have students make up a new ending to the story or a new turn to the basic idea. Television programs, Dear Abby-type columns, and movies can also be used as starting points.

These activities all encourage students to write their own ideas in their own words following an oral language activity. Fluency of expression will be developed; use of orally known words will reinforce previous oral language and reading activities. Figures 6-E through 6-I illustrate some compositions by Stage 2 students developing writing skills by using these kinds of stimuli.

*Figure 6-E*

*This story was written following discussion of the concept of a hero and one of the student's favorite television programs. This girl imagined herself to be the brave heroine.*

My favorite hero is
Bionic Woman because she is so
strong she helps everyone.

If I was bionic woman
I will help every one and if
a house was on fire I will get
everybody out of the house
and I will call the fire man.
So they could stop the fire
and when the fire stop everybody tell me thank you and
I said its nothing. Then I saw
a robber and I stopped him and
I said what did you have
in the bag nothing let me
see it its nothing O.K.
here and I saw 10,000.0 dollas
let me have it no. let me
have it no O.K. and I take it
to the jail and the
money I take it to the
Bank.

*Figure 6-F*

*These stories followed the reading and discussion of a story called "Cementing a Friendship." Each is a modified retelling of the basic story events.*

omce upon a time there
was a prety stret But one day
was an Earlhquake and
the stret cone down one day
a nan was paving the stret and
a litle gay was lost and He went
in the stret that it was wet when
the nan see at the little gay first

*Figure 6-F cont.*

The man get so mad But when he
mew was hapening he gat so sad
he take the boy to the Police and
live him Wait there But the litte gay
stare Crying and then the man
cone Back and ask him wait he
was crying the boy say I don't
have fanyly could I live with you
Of course said the man and
the boy whent to bed with
the man and now the litle goy
is a paber.

### Cementing a friend ship

Once upon a time there was an man
thath who likes to work paving the
side walk. Then a boy was walking trouy
the street and he saw a man paving
the street and the man saw the foot
print. And the man smile and the
man said to him self ho he is a little
Kid. then the man tell him what
you are doing here I was walking
trough the street and I am so sorry
becaruse I mix up your work thaths OK
did you want some ice cream sure.
Come on to the store and they
went to the store and they buy some
ice cream and so they aet the ice cream
the boy tooll the man he had to go
now O.K. I see you tomorrow O.K.
good by.

*Figure 6-G*

*This is an autobiographical account written by an eleven-year-old Chinese student.*

My family

I have a grandmother and grandfather. My grandfather is cook in a restaurant My father is a cook in a Chinese restaurant. My mother cleans room in a motel. My brother, Alexander goes to Bayside School. He is in the sixth grade. My sister, Mary goes to the Burlingame School She helps my mother cook.

*Figure 6-H*

*This is an account of a personal experience.*

on sunda I found a doller and I went to the store and spended fifty cents so I had fifty cents then I beted my brother that I cold run faster then hin from the park home and I lost and I lost fifty centc then he went to the store and I cutlent go becuse I dident have any money por me.

*Figure 6-1*

*These are three stories written by three different Stage 2 ESL students at
Halloween time.*

I got drest up like frenkingstin I wint
trachntriting and got some candy and went back hom
and ate it all up .

It is fun to go trickrtrite
backe yall get cande and cockes.
my Mom comes with me ond
it is nice to be withe her.

On hallowen I would like to be a wolf
to go all around the houses geting candy
with my friends and on the uay I uold
be eating candy some kids were mumys
and witches some of the houses lookd skery
to all the houses I went they had a
pumpkin on the door some of the hauses has
pumpkins with a kandle in them in some
houses people wernt in when my friends and
I got tird of geting candy, ue went home
and countid all the candy ue got and the
next day when ue uent to school ue take
some candy ate some in the uay and
sabed some for reses and some for lunch
and when ue got home ue got some more
candy the next day I uas gona get some
candy but they wernt were I puted them
and I knew my mom had goten them
becuse she dosent uant me to have cavetis
but my friends got candy and they gav
me some.

The student writing in Figures 6-D through 6-I reveal several typical errors Stage 2 students make in their writing. Some words are misspelled, and some phrasing is awkward or incorrect. Rather than being serious writing problems, these errors simply reveal the students' mastery of English at the time and should be used to assess progress in language development, not criticized. For instance, in "My Vacation" (Figure 6-D) the writer showed confusion over the sound of *d*, as evidenced by the encoding of *gay* and *gies* instead of *day* and *dies*. In fact, this student was still unable to discriminate these sounds auditorially, and the writing revealed the mix up. *Carry too much the puppy* also is an accurate recording of the way the child phrased this idea orally. Both stories about the workman and the boy (Figure 6-F) reveal similar writing errors stemming from the student's oral use of English as well as some confusion over encoding certain English sounds. One child had not mastered the spelling of *through* and *that's*, for example, while the other confused the use of *m* and *n,* writing *nan* for *man, mew* for *knew,* and *omce* for *once.*

These are all understandable errors, given the students' relatively recent exposure to English, with its often confusing and inconsistent spellings. In fact, it is more remarkable that these students were able to write as well as they did than that they made errors in their attempts. Actually, their writing reveals a good command of the language as well as lively, personal styles. Because their teachers encouraged them to write and accepted errors, the students learned to write confidently and fluently. One of the best indicators of their focus on communication rather than mechanical accuracy is the writing of *paving* at the beginning of one account (Figure 6-F) and *paber* (paver) at the end of the same account. The sounds of *v* and *b* are easily confused, and this boy had not yet learned to discriminate these sounds auditorially. However, the child was obviously more intent on communicating his meaning than on spelling words correctly, and so the inconsistency resulted.

As oral language skills increase, written language will show a corresponding improvement as long as production is not stifled by a premature emphasis on mechanical correctness. The prewriting and writing steps are still the most important at this stage, to encourage fluent expression of meaning, but when students are writing as well as those introduced in our examples, some revising and rewriting may be introduced.

Revision at Stage 2 should involve many opportunities to share writing and to hear the writing done by other students. Students may work in small groups to read aloud and discuss their work, attending to clarity of ideas expressed and the general effectiveness of the writing. Students should be encouraged to pay much attention to the strong points of their work so that each group member will maintain confidence in writing. As they read their writing aloud, students frequently notice and correct many errors orally, rephrasing statements correctly that they wrote incorrectly at first. Some students will also notice spelling errors as they read their work aloud; words that they have seen often in print, especially, may not look right to them when they see them misspelled. These changes may be easily incorporated in later drafts. Some students will ask directly for help in correcting their work, showing a readiness and confidence for recognizing their errors. Assistance should be provided matter-of-factly, emphasizing correcting for the purpose of improving communication effectiveness.

If consistent errors are made over time, these can be handled in separate lessons. For example, if students consistently confuse certain letters (such as *m* and *n* in our earlier example), these can be taught specifically. Or, if the same usage error appears in several writings (such as *carry too much the puppy*), lessons focusing on the particular problem can be planned. We want to emphasize that as oral language improves, written language will improve, and as students acquire greater sight vocabularies, greater command over sound/letter relationships, and increased reading ability, spelling and other mechanical elements of their writing skill will also improve naturally.

## WRITING FOR STAGE 3 STUDENTS

As students work with Stage 3 reading activities, a greater variety of composing tasks should be introduced so that students are exposed to written English in all its forms. Students at this stage are being exposed to a variety of other author reading materials, especially literature, and these models of written English may serve as stimuli for writing as well as dictation. Cooper (1981), for example, suggests that these literary forms serve as the foundation of a reading/writing program:

Poetry
Journals
Personal experience narratives
Fictional narratives
Drama
Reportage
Exposition
 Explanatory
 Persuasive
 Documented research

Giving students experience with different forms helps to emphasize that writing is primarily a form of communication, not simply an academic exercise. Different forms of writing can serve as models for students' own writing, expanding their ability to use writing for a variety of purposes.

When students model writing forms, it is often desirable to keep the topics personally meaningful. For instance, after hearing or reading and discussing the respective forms of literature, students might try writing activities like these:

1. Drama. Students write a play to portray their first few days of school, their move to their new home, or a typical activity they remember from their homeland.

2. Fictional narrative. Students write a story about a family moving from one country to another or a student making friends with new classmates.

3. Exposition - explanatory. Students enumerate and explain the problems a foreigner has when first moving to the U.S. or the difficulties encountered in learning to get along in a new culture.

4. Exposition - persuasive. Students write an essay to persuade readers of the value of seeking a new life or the difficulties of leaving an old one.

5. Exposition - documented research. Students write about their homeland, using newspaper articles or books to document various facts and descriptions, or they write their findings from an oral history project. (See page 59 for explanations of oral history projects as stimuli for dictation.)

Here are some compositions to illustrate Stage 3 writing. These learners were young adults attending a community college class to build English skills. Their assignment was to describe a special place, one with particular meaning to them. We have not altered spelling, usage, or mechanics.

> A special place that I like the most is a hill top called "EL VOLANTIN," it is located five milles from my home town up on the mountains, and it is one of the tallest around there, it looks like a piramid with a triangular flad rock sticking out of it, were I used to sit watching the little towns way down on the bottom, but the most I like was to watch the eagles fly and to watch the sunset. Wath I use to do was to sit at the edge of the rock with my fit hunging over the rock.
>
> By going there when I was a child helped me to enjoy and respect natural life, my feeling for this place haven't change and I hope will never change.

> I am going to talk about my house and surroundings in Japan. My house has a bed room, a

living room, two tatami rooms, a bath room, and a
kitchen. I like a tatami room very much. We can use it
sometimes a dining room, a bedroom, and a living room.
Also, I like smell of the tatami. The old Japanese
proverb said that a new tatami and a new wife is the best
thing. Do you agree? Also, the tatami room is quiet and
wide space, because furnitures are not suit in the tatami
room. The tatami was made of stem of rice and color is
light brown. In Japan, there are a plenty of stems,
because of rice country.

At the summer time, you can pick up many kind of
shells at the beach, a pink one which is look like baby's
hand, a blue one, a green one, etc. The air is nice too,
because of near the mountain. This is briefly explanation
about my house. Now, I am living in the U.S. that I
missed my house very much. If you will go to Japan,
please visit my house.

There is a small pleace in Mexico which I love very
much, is located an Michoacan state, about 3 hour away
of Guadalajar an 8 hour away of Mexico City, the name
of that town is call Santiago Tangamandapio, Mich. Is
look like a typical town of the cantry, but is not so agly
like that other, because is very clean and the people are
very friendly with all the people that goes to the town.
All the walls are white and the roofs is red is a tipical
colonlia town. It have one caffe chap and one tear in the
whole town and it have sevral stors, were you can go and
buy closse or go to la plazita. La plazita is very tipical
please in Mexico especial in that small towns like this
one were you can go and sit on a bench with your friend
on a afternoon Sanday which is very tipical to do that in
Mexico.

I live in Santiago Tangamandapio 13 year, all my
childhood a remember my friends and all my teacher and
school house were I used to play and got on fites with
my friend. Evey time a remember my town a get
melancolic.

My badroom is the place which has particular
meaning for me. My badroom is not too big. It is small
and comfortable. On one of the walls I have my bad,
and two pictures ganging on the wall. On the other wall
there is a window that I can watch people walkins on the

street. In other of the walls I have my stereo, and one picture ganging of the wall which has a lot of meaning for me.

My badroom it is the place where I like to be most of my free time. It is the place where I like to do my homework, or lisent miucic. It is the place where I like to think what I did, or what I want to do. In conclusion my badroom is the place which has particular meaning for me, and I like to pass most of my free time.

I'am going to describe my home town. My home town is Tehran. Tehran is captial of Iran.

Tehran is a big city excitly the seem L.A. It has a lot of factory, company, hospital, college, university, school, church, store and big and big building.

The people in my home town are very friendly with each other. Always they helping each other. They are very honest.

The life in Tehran is start at 7:00 in the morning until 12 PM and the people are very activity.

I born in Tehran and I lived there for 19 years.

One hundred years ago, Hong Kong was still a poor city. There were not many people lived, because there were not much chance to looked for jobs, most of the residents were the fishermen, operated on the ocean, some worked in the farms. Their lifes were so quiet and peaceful, lived in the nature and beautiful island. But today's Hong Kong, such like the big cities around the world, modernize tall buildings align the streets. You would feel that you are in the valley when walk in the city, the traffic are busy at any time except in the midnight. Terrible pollution makes people sick. A few years ago, although Hong Kong's government constructed subway for transit, but there are still has a lot of problem for traffic, because too many people live in the small island. When Sunday or holidays, people walk in the streets just like the waves move in the ocean. Many people rather stay in home instead go out when holiday. Although Hong Kong has many problems, but Hong Kong is such amacing place, he has huge energy to proceed forward, there are change everyday. Couble months ago I saw a TV show was intorduce about Hong Kong, they said Hong Kong is a great city. They though

> New York City is a greatest city of the world before they
> went to Hong Kong, but now they are change their mine.

At this stage writing confidence and fluency will become well
established. Students will be able to pay more attention to revising their
writing not only to improve clarity but also to correct errors in usage and
mechanics. Of course, spelling, vocabulary, and sentence structure will
continue to improve naturally with continued work on oral language and
reading skills. In fact, with every opportunity to speak, hear, or read
English, students improve their abilities to write English. Simply
correcting errors as they occur in writing will do less to improve written
expression as such correction is generally, as Collins (1980) points out, a
"change which we actively control and the student passively accepts."
Rather, oral and written expression need to be integrated, as Collins
further suggests, "interactive, not counteractive." This is a particularly
important principle in helping Stage 3 students revise their writing since,
for these students, all aspects of communication in English are especially
reinforcing to one another.

Revisions can best be accomplished by first having students work
together in groups, sharing their writing with one another by reading
pieces aloud and discussing good points as well as suggested revisions, as
was done with Stage 2 students. Each student's increasing ability with
English will contribute unique strengths to the group effort; Stage 3
sharing groups will often be able to suggest good revisions in phrasing,
usage, vocabulary, and sentence structure as well as desirable changes in
the content of the writing. English-speaking classmates may also be
included in these groups and will be a good resource for the ESL
students. Students will be able to help each other a good deal at this
point, even if they do not note and correct all of the errors in their work,
and this process for revising should be used to integrate the act of writing
with the reading and oral language practice the students are continuing to
receive.

More detailed revisions can best be accomplished, as students are
ready, by following the same procedures outlined in Chapter 4 for
revising dictated stories. Student and teacher work together through the
composition, revising statements and correcting errors as they are noted.
In addition, time may be spent dealing with frequently occurring errors in
separate lessons, through planned activities that are closely related to
oral/aural and reading tasks. For instance, several statements with the
same usage problem may be collected from different writings to be
discussed and revised in one lesson. Or usage errors noted in writing may
be used as the basis for oral language lessons. For example, here is a
composition done by Jose, a Stage 3 student, and the revision that was
done with teacher help.

> Good health is very important to me because If you
> are not in good health When you come to in every class
> you are almost sleep and that is why you need a good
> health The things you can do for a good health are — to
> eat good food with a lot of colories and vitamines and
> not for be with your friends in the movies don't sleep,
> you have to sleep the time that is goo for your health.

### The Gift of Health

> Good health is very important to me because if I am
> not in good health when I come to school in  every class
> I fall asleep. That is why I need to be healthy. The things
> I can do to keep myself healthy are to eat good food
> with a lot of vitamins and get enough sleep and exercise.

The revisions were made after rereading the composition and discussing certain awkward phrasings and choice of words. After pointing out areas in need of work and showing better ways to state the ideas, the teacher had Jose talk about the ideas again before going back to revise the paper. Spelling errors were corrected quickly by the teacher and were not presented as a major problem with the writing. During the discussion, Jose decided on his own to revise the content of the composition, leaving out some ideas he had originally included and adding some new things. The revised composition reflects the corrections and changes made with this kind of individualized help.

Of course, good preparation before writing will usually cut down the amount of time spent revising a composition. Stage 3 students should especially be encouraged to organize their thoughts before they begin to write, thinking through what they want to say and how they want to say it in advance. Figure 6-J illustrates a detailed cluster outline done by a Stage 3 student and the final version of her composition. Because she had spent time thinking and organizing before writing, her first draft required little revision, and her final composition reflects good ideas and good language usage.

Stage 3 students are not only learning to write but are also engaged in writing to learn; they are expected to complete writing assignments in various content classes. Writing activities are thus an integral part of the students' total instructional program at this point, including the kind of writing required in their other classes. The same stimuli used for Stage 3 dictation (see page 56) may also be used for encouraging writing at this stage. Just as students can dictate mathematics story problems, steps in science experiments, or summaries of historical events, they can also write these ideas to supplement their learning. Notetaking and homework assignments can be stressed as well as other subject-related assignments.

Figure 6-J

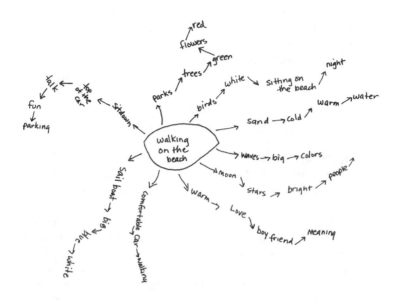

The Beach at Night

I think walking on the beach is fun because you see white birds sitting on the beach at night. When you touch the water, it's warm but the sand is a little bit cold. The waves are big. The water has many colors. The moon and stars are bright.

People watch the stars and the moon; boy friends and girl friends are together, thinking about the meaning of life. It's comfortable watching everything from the car or while walking. You can also see a lot of sailboats on the beach.

Some structured activities can also be included in the Stage 3 program to help students further refine writing skills. By structured writing we mean writing tasks designed specifically to develop better use of language structures and vocabulary. Structured writing can encourage students to manipulate the language along various dimensions and thereby gain greater control over written expression. For example, Paulston (1978) recommends a number of "controlled composition" activities which can help ESL students purposefully manipulate English by making a variety of conversions while rewriting a given text. These suggestions are adapted from some of those mentioned in her work.

1. Have students rewrite paragraphs in which simple substitutions are required. For example, this paragraph can be rewritten substituting *Joe* for *Sue* and *Princess* for *Prince*. All pronouns referring to these two nouns must also be changed accordingly; only one change is possible in each instance.

> Sue came to school one day with her dog, Prince. Prince
> could do lots of tricks. He could jump over Sue's arm
> and sit by her side. He could roll over and play dead.
> Everyone loved Prince and his tricks.

2. Have students rewrite paragraphs requiring more complex substitutions. For example, this paragraph can be rewritten to describe a summer day instead of a winter day. There are a variety of substitutions that may be used to convey the new meaning.

> It was very cold outside. The sky was gray, and the
> temperature was 39°. The sun was not shining; it was
> dreary and wet. People wore sweaters and heavy coats to
> keep warm. Nothing tasted so good as a hot bowl of
> soup on that day!

3. Have students rewrite a paragraph by combining short, simple sentences into sentences of greater complexity. For example, the sentences in this paragraph can be combined in various way to improve the overall effect. See Cooper (1976) for other sentence combining activities.

> The man was walking down the street. The man was very
> old. A dog walked with him. The dog was very old too.
> The man carried a cane. He moved slowly. He stopped
> often to rest. He wore a brown coat. He also wore a
> brown hat.

4. Have students expand paragraphs to include a greater number of descriptive words or phrases. For example, any number of words may be added to this paragraph to elaborate the description.

> The _____, _____ girl was playing in the park
> with her _____, _____ brother. They ran and
> jumped _____. Soon, some other _____,
> _____ children came along and they all played
> together _____ and _____.

For each of these structured activities, the original piece of writing should be taken from dictated stories or from familiar reading materials. Special paragraphs may also be written for the students, using familiar words and ideas.

Other strategies may combine a certain amount of structure with imaginative ideas to refine language skills in unique ways. For instance,

Pradl (1979) has suggested an interesting way of helping students write poetry which may be adapted for the Stage 3 student. The basic steps are:

1. List key words from a poem in a single column.

2. Have students write an association for each word next to the original word. (An association should be the first word the students think of when they read the original word.)

3. Give students the original poem, with blanks where the listed words appeared.

4. Have students fill in the blanks with the new words (their associations).

This exercise will result in a new poem, which can be compared with the intact original. Interesting discussions of word choice, word function, and shifts in meaning will result as students compare poems. Vocabulary and written expression will also be reinforced. (Also see Christison, 1982.)

Overall, writing activities for the Stage 3 student need to extend and refine the language that is encountered in oral exchanges and through reading. The emphasis is on expressing meaning; revising and rewriting can help students correct usage and mechanical errors. The activities we have suggested are only a few possibilites. The Stage 3 student is probably most like the successful native English-speaking student who takes a foreign language course: for both these students, the background of reading and writing in the native language makes reading and writing in the new language relatively easy to handle as long as the learning activities are reinforcing to one another. Stage 3 students should be able to handle a wide variety of writing tasks in English; individual programs should be planned according to the interests and academic needs of the student.

## SUMMARY

LEA writing programs for ESL students are based on principles of the composing process. Activities are related to oral language and reading activities so as to reinforce language in all areas. For students at each stage, writing instruction is consistent with the kind of dictation and oral/aural work appropriate for that stage. Emphasis is placed on having students see writing as a form of communication. They share their work with one another to (a) orally supplement the written communication to complete getting the message across and (b) to discover what would strengthen their written presentation without the anxiety of harsh error correction from an authority figure. Corrections and revisions are made in different ways, depending on the student's level of competence in writing and self-confidence in handling writing tasks.

# REFERENCES

Britton, J. *Language and Learning*. Harmonsworth, England: Penguin, 1970.

Caplan, R., & Keech, C. *Showing-Writing: A Training Program to Help Students Be Specific*. Berkeley: University of California, Bay Area Writing Project, 1980.

Christison, M.A. *English Through Poetry*. San Francisco: The Alemany Press, 1982.

Christison, M.A., & Bassano, S. *Look Who's Talking!* San Francisco: The Alemany Press, 1981.

Collins, J.L. *Speaking and writing: The semantic connection*. Paper presented at the English Education Conference, Omaha, Nebraska: ERIC REPORTS: ED 185 561, 1980.

Cooper, C. An outline for writing sentence combining problems. In Graves, R., *Rhetoric and Composition: A Sourcebook*, Rochelle Park, NJ: Hayden, 1976.

Cooper, C. *Experiments with discourse guides*. Paper presented at the South Coast Writing Project, University of California, Santa Barbara, July, 1981.

Dennis, J., Griffin, S., & Wills, R. *English Through Drama*. San Francisco: The Alemany Press, 1981.

Elbow, P. *Writing Without Teachers*. New York: Oxford University Press, 1973.

Hanf, M.B. "Mapping: A technique for translating reading into thinking." *Journal of Reading*, January, 1971, 225-304.

Martin, N., D'Arcy, P., Newton, B., & Parker, R. *Writing and Learning Across the Curriculum 11-16*. London: Ward Lock Educational, 1976.

Moffett, J. *Active Voice: A Writing Program Across the Curriculum*. Montclair, NJ: Boynton/Cook, 1981.

Moffett, J. *Teaching the Universe of Discourse*. New York: Houghton Mifflin, 1968.

Myers, M. *A Model for the Composing Process*. Berkeley: University of California, Bay Area Writing Project, 1980.

Olsen, J.E. W-B. *Communication Starters*. San Francisco: The Alemany Press, 1977.

Paulston, C.B. "Teaching writing in the ESOL classroom: Techniques of controlled composition." In *Reading and Writing*, Albany: New York State Education Department, 1978.

Pradl, G.M. *Expectation and Cohesion*. Berkeley: University of California, Bay Area Writing Project, 1979.

Rico, G.L. & Claggett, M.F. *Balancing the Hemispheres: Brain Research and the Teaching of Writing*. Berkeley: University of California, Bay Area Writing Project, 1980.

Riverol, A. *The Action Reporter*. San Francisco: The Alemany Press, 1984.

Seward, B. *Writing American English*. San Francisco: The Alemany Press, 1982.

# Chapter 7

# One Teacher's Class

The basic LEA steps we have outlined can be further adapted to suit the needs of a particular group. One good example of such a modification occurred in a special program for ESL students.* Three children, an eleven-year-old Chinese girl and a Vietnamese brother and sister, ten and seven respectively, entered the school in September without any oral English abilties, that is, as Stage 1 students. From the first of the year they, along with other, similar students, were given extensive oral language activities to help them understand their teachers and fellow students and to help them express themselves in school. They learned basic vocabulary used in school so they could follow simple directions and talk about school activities and common classroom objects. By January, the Chinese girl and the Vietnamese siblings were communicating rather easily in English and thus were ready to learn to read words they were using orally. They were grouped together because they had made similar progress in the oral language program and because it seemed they would be able to function well as a group. As their reading instruction began, they continued their oral language training, and the two components of the program reinforced one another.

The teacher decided to use LEA principles to get the students started reading English and was first concerned about finding appropriate stimuli for dictation. Knowing the children's fascination with animals, the teacher showed the group a book filled with close-up colored photographs of different kinds of baby animals. The group chose pictures they liked, and these became the basis for their first dictated stories. The teacher asked questions to get the students to look carefully at the pictures and describe the animals and their surroundings. At first the children were not sure

*We thank Sandra Coopersmith-Beezy, ESL teacher, San Mateo, CA for telling us about her LEA program and allowing us to describe it here and use samples of her students' work for illustration.

what to say, but with encouraging questions they soon learned to talk freely about the animals. The teacher recorded their statements, and these dictated accounts became the basic reading materials for the group.

If a student dictated a statement that did not conform to regular English usage, the teacher immediately corrected the statement orally and wrote it in the story in its corrected form. This was done so that from the start the story would be a good model of English usage as it was used for reading instruction. Although the students were really Stage 2 students, whose English would not, according to our guidelines, be corrected, this modification seemed appropriate for two reasons. First, the students were eager to learn standard English usage, often asked if their statements were correct, and were not offended or frustrated with the teacher's corrections. Second, the Vietnamese children were taking their schoolwork home to share with their parents, who were also just learning to speak and read English. The teacher believed the Vietnamese family should have good models of English to use as they learned with their children since they had few other contacts with English speakers.

Because of the extensive oral language training early in the school year, few corrections were actually needed in the dictated stories. Most often the teacher needed to call attention to misused or omitted prepositions, subject-verb agreement, and relatively minor deviations from standard English. The essential ideas and sentence structure of the children were maintained when their dictation was recorded. Two of the group's earliest stories, based on the animal photographs, were "Fish" and "Meow the Kitten." Both are given here as they were after corrections had been made.

### Fish

Fish live in the ocean. This fish is red. We eat fish. I like fish. The fish is big and the fish is small.

### Meow the Kitten

The eyes are circles. The kitten is brown. The eyes are yellow and black. The ears are big. The paw is white. The kitten is cute. I like cats.

During the dictation of these and later stories, the teacher supplied English words when the children obviously wanted to use a word but did not know the English equivalent. For instance, one child began the statement, "Fish live in the . . ." and indicated by pointing to the water in the picture and by sweeping gestures that he meant ocean, so the teacher supplied that word. In the kitten story, another child said, "The . . . is white" while pointing to the cat's paw and looking questioningly at the teacher, who then supplied the word paw.

At first the dictated stories included short, simple statements that reflected the language patterns the children had been learning with their oral English activities. These early accounts also reflected some of the English vocabulary the children had been learning in their oral program. For instance, in "Meow the Kitten" the use of circles to describe the cat's eyes seemed to result directly from a recent oral language exercise which stressed English words for different geometric shapes.

The teacher also made judicious use of an English-Vietnamese dictionary on some occasions. For instance, in the kitten story, one Vietnamese child dictated "The kitten is nice" but seemed dissatisfied with the word nice as a descriptor. The teacher suggested the word cute, which was unfamiliar to the group. They all looked up the Vietnamese equivalent of cute in the dictionary, and the child who had dictated the statement agreed at once, after hearing the Vietnamese word, that cute was just the word she wanted. This tactic was used only occasionally with the Vietnamese children and not at all with the Chinese girl because, unfortunately, an English-Chinese dictionary was unavailable. The teacher was careful not to suggest any alternative English words, of course, unless there seemed to be a real desire for a better word. (This occasional comparison of English and Vietnamese sometimes proved amusing as well as enlightening. For instance, the group discovered to their surprise that while "meow" is the Vietnamese word for cat, it is also the English word for the sound made by cats. The title "Meow the Kitten" reflected their delight at this discovery.) Ordinarily, translation from English to the native language, to aid meaning, is not advisable because translation can too easily become a crutch, delaying acquisition of English. Used sparingly with this group, however, the tactic worked well.

Thus, by asking good questions, correcting awkward English phrasing, and supplying needed words, the teacher helped the group talk about the animal pictures in English and construct a dictated account that capitalized on known English words and phrases and also reflected their ideas and concepts about the animal.

As the group dictated stories from week to week, they reused many words they had used in earlier stories, reinforcing their speaking and reading vocabularies. Their dictations gradually became longer, including more variety in vocabulary and, to some extent, sentence structure. The following stories show this growth over a period of several weeks. All were dictated in response to group discussion and observation of animal pictures from the same book.

### The Little Deer

The nose is black. The deer lives in the jungle. His ear is
big. His eyes are black. His face is yellow. He is looking

at the flowers. The flowers are blue and pink. The plants
are green. He is very cute.

### The Butterfly

The butterfly is cute. She likes flowers. She is on the
flower. The butterfly is many different colors. The girl is
looking at the butterfly. The nose is little. She lives in
the air.

### The Leopard

This is a leopard. He has eyes. The leopard has spots.
His paws are brown. His eyes are green. His ears are
little. He lives in a cave. His mouth is big.

### Birds

The baby birds are hungry. The birds are black. The
mouth is wide. They live in the nest. The nest is in the
tree. The bird is little.

Once the children had dictated a story, which was recorded on the
chalkboard, they were asked to copy the story in their story books.
Although we have not recommended that Stage 2 students copy their
own stories, the plan worked well in this group. All three children could
form words easily and clearly and were able to copy the story in a few
minutes. The copies of the stories in Figure 7-1 illustrate the good
handwriting of the seven- and nine-year-old children. They and the other
child found the activity easy to do and satisfying although the teacher
was prepared to provide copies for them if the task became too difficult.

*Figure 7-1*

Birds

The baby birds are hungry.
The birds are black.
The mouth is wide.
They live in the nest.
The nest is in the tree.
The bird is little.

The eyes are circles.
The Kitten is brown.
The eyes are yellow and
black. The ears are big
The paw is white.
The Kitten is cute.
I like cats.

During the week the group reread their story many times, either together as a group or individually. The teacher supplied unknown words during these readings to maintain the fluency of the reading. Also, the group devoted a good deal of time over several days reinforcing their knowledge of individual words in the story. The teacher put the story words, in scrambled order, on the chalkboard and asked the students to point out different words. This also reinforced oral language exercises they were doing at other times during the day. For instance, for several weeks the group was working on common prepositions such as under, over, beside, around. The teacher reinforced this learning by asking the children to identify story words by going to the board and putting a star beside a certain word or drawing a line under another word. These regular word practice activities proved sufficient to reinforce the children's learning of story words. Sequential and Scrambled Lists and Word Banks were not used since they did not seem necessary for additional reinforcement. The children were encouraged, however, to take their stories home regularly, and, in the case of the Vietnamese siblings, the whole family read the stories together and practiced identifying words from the stories.

After the animal pictures in the special book had been used quite thoroughly, new dictation topics were needed. The teacher began using other stimuli for dictation as interesting things happened to the children or as the teacher found things to bring to the class. One day the teacher brought a salamander to the group, a creature that intrigued the children. On another occasion the Vietnamese children reported having moved into a new house, and their experiences were used as the topic of another story. These two stories are reproduced here. They illustrate the growing control over English vocabulary and sentence structure as well as the children's ability to describe in English more than the concrete, immediate features of the previously-used pictures.

### The Salamander

Mrs. Beezey brings a salamander to school. We hold the salamander in our hand. She is walking on my hand. She is crawling on Hai's hand. She lives in the water and the mud. Mrs. Beezey put it in the glass. The salamander eats bugs. We like the salamander.

### The New House

The new house is big. The new house has four bedrooms and two bathrooms. The house is pink. The new house has swings. The back yard is big. There is grass in back and in front of the house. The tree is high. The tree is in the back yard. The house is very, very old. We like the big new house.

During these months the teacher also used colorful pictures of various family scenes that reflected a number of typically American activities. These stimuli encouraged the group to use their quickly increasing English vocabulary to describe the people and objects in the pictures. Three of these stories illustrate the continuing growth in the group's ability to use varied vocabulary and sentences.

### The Family

The family is at the table. The girl is sad because she can't play. Outside it is raining. The girl is eating fruits and food. There are apples and bananas and meat and eggs and pie and milk on the table. The cat is sitting on the chair and looking at the plate. She wants to eat.

### The Children and Hot Dogs

The children are walking to eat. They see a table. They have a box. The box is in the boy's hand. The children

are cooking hot dogs. The boy has glasses. They are
hungry. The children are eating the hot dogs on the
table. They are drinking 7-Up. The children are on the
beach. The children are putting garbage in the garbage
can. They are happy.

### The Clean Dog

The girl is putting the water in the bucket. The girl is
putting the dog in the water. She is washing the dog.
The dog is shaking the water. The dog is clean. The girl
is wet. The bucket is big. The girl is brushing the dog.
The dog is clean. She is happy.

At times the topics for dictation followed directly from various oral
language activities. One day, knowing the children were still having some
difficulty using prepositions and other direction words, the teacher
decided to focus on these troublesome words. Teacher and students
moved in various ways to illustrate certain terms, and they all practiced
making different statements using the words. The story that resulted was
called "The Funny Story" by the group because it was a collection of
these seemingly unrelated statements, an atypical story for the group.

### The Funny Story

I go across the street. Mrs. Beezey dances forward. She
looks happy. I walk backwards to the classroom. I am
silly. A dog is underneath the table. He is sleeping. We
walk sideways in a line. We look happy.

Almost every day a teacher, aide, or student would bring something
special into the classroom for sharing time. These events also served as
good stimuli for dictations once the group became used to the dictating
process. "Mille the Rabbit" illustrates a story obtained on one such
occasion.

### Mille the Rabbit

Mrs. Ackerman brings the rabbit to school and shares it
with everybody. The rabbit has long ears and a little tail.
The rabbit is brown. Its stomach is white. The rabbit
eats a cooky, and a carrot, and parsley. She jumps on
the cage and around the classroom. Mrs. Ackerman tied
a pink ribbon on the rabbit's ears. We like the rabbit.
The rabbit is cute.

One of the last stories of the school year followed a discussion of ghosts, stimulated by a vivid television program that all had seen. The improvement in this late spring story shows the children's growth since September, when they were not speaking any English, and since January, when they first began dictating simple stories. The story reflects personal experiences of two of the children as well as some of the ideas discussed by the group.

### The Ghost Scares Loan

On Halloween the ghosts scare everybody. I've never
seen a ghost. Some people say ghosts are not real. The
ghost scared Loan last night and early this morning.
Once on the island Hai was afraid of ghosts. At night he
couldn't sleep.

Once the children began making good progress with their dictated stories, some time in April, the teacher encouraged them to begin writing their own stories as well. One activity stimulated much interest at this time. The children watched films of a popular monster character and then read accompanying books that told the same stories. Finally, they wrote their own stories, retelling the film/book events. The teacher read each story with the student and helped make corrections in English usage. The student then recopied the story on fresh paper and put it in the story book for later sharing with family and friends. One of these monster stories is illustrated here:

*Figure 7-2*

The Monster Story

The monster goes to the city and he goes
on the bus. He told the children to
go to the school park. Then he climbed
the street light. He looked at the
city. Then he went to the clothing store.
Then he went to the house to
sleep.

Other stories were written on a variety of topics. Here are two stories from this group, written in response to pictures shown by the teacher.

*Figure 7-3*

The Family and the Plane

The family is eating by the lake.

The boy is playing with the plane.

The boy is sad because the plane goes down in the water. His father tries to get the plane. He didn't get it. The dog swims to the plane and gives it to the boy. The boy is happy. His father cleans the plane.

The Men and the truck

The men get off the truck to drink coffee. Another man is stealing the truck. The men are yelling, "Help!, Help!" They are taking another car to chase the man who took their truck. The policeman arrested the thief. The men are happy and they drive the truck away.

The end

The teacher noted that these stories, and other student-written stories, showed more limited vocabulary and sentence structure than the dictated stories were showing at the same time. It was clear that although the students quite enjoyed writing their own stories, it was still a more difficult task than dictating. Student-written stories were a good supplement to the program, but dictated stories had not lost their value for developing language fluency and reading skills.

Since the students enjoyed writing, the teacher suggested they keep journals during the spring vacation. They were quite enthusiastic about the assignment. When they returned from the week's holiday, each had a journal of daily activities. These entries illustrate part of this work. The writing is presented in its uncorrected form.

Saturday   I am staying at home and watching at the TV
           and I am playing backyard my swings.

Sunday     I went to church after that went home and
           played with my sister and my brother.

Monday     I went to park and played with my cousin my
           sister and my brother after that come back and
           study English.

The teacher worked with each student, making needed corrections and praising fine efforts. Though some language awkwardness is still evident, it is clear that the students had made excellent progress since September, when they had arrived in school unable to speak, much less write, any English.

We give this example to stress the flexibility of LEA for working with ESL students. Classroom circumstances and specific student needs should determine when our procedures may need to be modified. This teacher chose to place somewhat more emphasis on correcting usage because the students were using their stories at home. Word recognition practice was done at the board, without use of Sequential and Scrambled Lists and Word Banks, and children made their own copies of their stories. These modifications were appropriate for the students in the group.

What were not changed were the basic principles of the approach. Dictation resulted from discussion of topics which were personally meaningful and interesting to the students. Stories were read and reread, and the story words were reinforced daily. The LEA reading program complemented continuing oral language work, and writing was introduced to reinforce both; the program involved all the communication skills. Most important, the reading materials directly represented the students' current levels of English skills. As their English improved, their stories became more detailed and better expressed.

Growth in reading ability occurred naturally as the students became more able users of English. In short, the program matched student needs and rates of learning while providing a non-threatening and effective way of learning to read.

# BIBLIOGRAPHY

Asher, J.J. *Learning Another Language Through Actions.* Los Gatos, CA: Sky Oaks Productions, 1977.

Ashton-Warner, S. *Teacher.* New York: Simon and Schuster, 1963.

Britton, J. *Language and Learning.* Harmonsworth, England: Penguin, 1970.

Brown, H.D. The seventies: Learning to ask the right questions. *Language Learning,* June 1979, *29,* v-vi.

Brown, R. *A First Language: The Early Stages.* Cambridge: Harvard University Press, 1973.

Brown, R., & Hanlon, C. Derivational complexity and order of acquisition. In Hays, J. (Ed.), *Cognition and the Development of Language,* New York: J. Wiley, 1970, 11-53.

Burns, P.C., & Roe, B.D. *Reading Activities for Today's Elementary Schools.* Chicago: Rand McNally, 1979.

Calvert, J.D. *Language experience as an affective and cognitive mobilizer to learning in the secondary classroom.* Paper presented at the 8th Conference of the California Reading Association, San Diego, 1974.

Caplan, R., & Keech, C. *Showing-Writing: A Training Program to Help Students Be Specific.* Berkeley: University of California, Bay Area Writing Project, 1980.

Ching, D.C. *Reading and the Bilingual Child.* Newark, DE: International Reading Association, 1976.

Christison, M.A. *English Through Poetry.* San Francisco: The Alemany Press, 1982.

_____ & Bassano, S. *Look Who's Talking!* San Francisco: The Alemany Press, 1981.

Collins, J.L. *Speaking and writing: The semantic connection.* Paper presented at the English Education Conference, Omaha, Nebraska: ERIC REPORTS: ED 185 561, 1980.

Cooper, C. An outline for writing sentence combining problems. In Graves, R., *Rhetoric and Composition: A Sourcebook,* Rochelle Park, NJ: Hayden, 1976.

_____ , *Experiments with discourse guides.* Paper presented at the South Coast Writing Project, University of California, Santa Barbara, July, 1981.

Dennis, J., Griffin, S., & Wills, R. *English Through Drama.* San Francisco: The Alemany Press, 1981.

Elbow, P. *Writing Without Teachers.* New York: Oxford University Press, 1973.

Elkins, R.J., & Bruggemann, C. *Comic strips in the teaching of English as a foreign language.* Paper presented to a conference on the teaching of English, Kassel, West Germany: ERIC REPORTS: ED 056 591, February, 1971.

Fowles, J. Ho, ho, ho: Cartoons in the language class. *TESOL Quarterly,* June, 1970, *4,* 155-160.

Goodman, K., & Fleming, J., (Eds.). *Psycholinguistics and the Teaching of Reading.* Newark, DE: International Reading Association, 1968.

Hall, G.E., & Loucks, S.F. A developmental model for determining whether the treatment is actually implemented. *American Educational Research Journal,* Summer 1977, *14,* 253-276.

Hall, G.E., Loucks, S.F., Rutherford, W.L., & Newlove, B.W. Levels of use of the innovation: A framework for analyzing innovation adoption. *Journal of Teacher Education,* Spring 1975, *26,* 52-56.

Hanf, M.B. Mapping: A technique for translating reading into thinking. *Journal of Reading,* January, 1971, 225-304.

Hartley, W.G., & Shumway, G.L. *An Oral History Primer.* Salt Lake City: The Author's Box, 1973.

Hirsch, R., & Lewinger, M. Oral history: The family is the curriculum. *Teacher,* November, 1975, 93, 60-62.

Horne, C. *Word Weaving: A Storytelling Workbook.* San Francisco: The Zellerbach Family Fund, 1980.

Huey, E.B. *The Psychology and Pedagogy of Reading.* New York: Macmillan, 1908.

Kettering, J.C. *Developing Communication Competence: Interaction Activities in English as a Second Language.* Pittsburgh: University of Pittsburgh Center for International Studies, 1975.

Krashen, S.D. *Second Language Acquisition,* Oxford: The Pergamon Press, 1981.

Krashen, S.D., & Terrell, T.D. *The Natural Approach.* San Francisco: The Alemany Press, 1983.

La Puma, L. *How Language is Learned: First and Second Language Acquisition.* Unpublished M.A. Thesis, University of California at Santa Barbara, 1981.

Lamoreaux, L., & Lee, D.M. *Learning to Read Through Experiences.* New York: Appleton-Century-Crofts, 1943.

Martin, N., D'Arcy, P., Newton, B., & Parker, R. *Writing and Learning Across the Curriculum 11-16.* London: Ward Lock Educational, 1976.

Moffett, J. *Active Voice: A Writing Program Across the Curriculum.* Montclair, NJ: Boynton/Cook, 1981.

_____ , *Teaching the Universe of Discourse.* New York: Houghton Mifflin, 1968.

Morley, H.J., & Lawrence, M.S. The use of films in teaching English as a second language. *Language and Learning,* June, 1971, *22,* 117-135.

_____ , The use of films in teaching English as a second language. *Language and Learning,* June, 1977, *22,* 99-110.

Myers, M. *A Model for the Composing Process.* Berkeley: University of California, Bay Area Writing Project, 1980.

Nelson, K. *Structure and Strategy in Learning to Talk.* Monographs of the Society for Research in Child Development, Seriel No. 149 1-2, 1973, *38,* 1-137.

Nessel, D.D., & Jones, M.B. *The Language-Experience Approach to Reading: A Handbook for Teachers.* New York: Teachers College Press, 1981.

Neuenschwander, J. *Oral History as a Teaching Approach.* Washington, D.C.: National Education Association, 1976.

Olsen, J.E. W-B. *Communication-Starters*. San Francisco: The Alemany Press, 1977.

Paulston, C.B. Teaching writing in the ESOL classroom: Techniques of controlled composition. In *Reading and Writing*, Albany: New York State Education Department, 1978.

Pradl, G.M. *Expectation and Cohesion*. Berkeley: University of California, Bay Area Writing Project, 1979.

Ransom, G. *Preparing to Teach Reading*. Boston: Little, Brown, 1978.

Rico, G.L., & Claggett, M.F. *Balancing the Hemispheres: Brain Research and the Teaching of Writing*. Berkeley: University of California, Bay Area Writing Project, 1980.

Riverol, A. *The Action Reporter*. San Francisco: The Alemany Press, 1984.

Roe, B.D., Stoodt, B.D. & Burns, P.C. *Reading Instruction in the Secondary School*. Chicago: Rand McNally, 1978.

St. Martin, G.M. *Films in the ESL Classroom*. Paper presented at the annual conference of the National Association for Foreign Student Affairs, Iowa State University, ERIC REPORTS: ED 159 916, June, 1978.

Saville-Troike, M. *Foundations for Teaching English as a Second Language: Theory and Method*. Englewood Cliffs, N.J.: Prentice Hall, 1976.

Schmelter, H. Teaching English to Mexican American students. *Today's Education*. March, 1972, *61*, 41.

Seward, B. *Writing American English*. San Francisco: The Alemany Press, 1982.

Shuy, R., (Ed.). *Linguistic Theory: What Can It Say About Reading?* Newark, DE: International Reading Association, 1967.

Smith, N.B. *American Reading Instruction*. Newark, DE: International Reading Association, 1967.

Spache, E. *Reading Activities for Child Involvement*. Boston: Allyn and Bacon, 1976.

Spache, G.E., & Spache, E.B. *Reading in the Elementary School*. Boston: Allyn and Bacon, 1977.

Stauffer, R.G. *The Language Experience Approach to the Teaching of Reading*. New York: Harper and Row, 1980.

_____ , Abrams, J.C., & Pikulski, J.J. *Diagnosis, Correction, and Prevention of Reading Disabilities*. New York: Harper and Row, 1978.

Swain, E.H. Using comic books to teach reading and language arts. *Journal of Reading*, December, 1978, *22*, 255-258.

Tierney, R.J., Readence, J.E., & Dishner, E.K. *Reading Strategies and Practices: A Guide for Improving Instruction*. Boston: Allyn and Bacon, 1980.

Trager, E.C. *PD's in Depth: Pronunciation/Aural Discrimination Drills for Learners of English*. Culver City, CA: ELS Publications, 1982, xvi-xxi.

Veatch, J., Sawicki, F., Elliot, G., Flake, E., & Blakey, J. *Key Words to Reading: The Language Experience Approach Begins*. Columbus: Charles Merrill, 1979.

Wilson, R.M., & Hall, M. *Reading and the Elementary School Child*. New York: D. Van Nostrand, 1972.